COUNTRIES OF THE WORLD

Liberia

Gareth Stevens Publishing
A WORLD ALMANAC EDUCATION GROUP COMPANY

About the Author: Paul Rozario is a graduate of Oxford and London universities. A professional writer and editor specializing in African titles, He has lived and worked in East Africa and has written and edited books on Kenya, Tunisia, and Nigeria.

PICTURE CREDITS
Agence France Presse: 13, 37, 60 (top), 72, 73, 83, 84
Paul Alsmay/Corbis: 1
Bettmann/Corbis: 10, 78
Camera Press Ltd: 39
The Coca-Cola Company: 85
Corbis: 1, 6, 9, 10, 44, 45, 50, 54, 77, 78, 79, 81
Getty Images/Hulton Archive: 11, 12, 14, 15 (bottom), 23, 26, 48, 51, 55, 62, 63, 80, 82
iAfrika: 4, 18, 20 (left and right), 21, 27, 42, 68, 69, 74, 87, 89
Bernt Karlsson: 29, 38, 56, 57, 70, 91
Martin Klejnowski Kennedy: 17, 22
Karen E. Lange: 3 (center), 7, 8, 16 (bottom), 24, 34, 36, 40, 41, 43, 61, 76
The Language Museum: 53
Lonely Planet Images: 33 (top), 46, 47
Online Liberia: 71
Dawn Padmore: 30
Panos Pictures: cover, 16 (top), 60 (bottom)
Won-Ldy Paye: 59
Philadelphia Zoo: 15 (top), 67 (left and right)
Albrecht G. Schaefer/Corbis: 6, 9
Liba Taylor: 28, 32
Still Pictures: 5, 25, 31, 35, 66
Topham Picturepoint: 2, 3 (top), 19, 64, 65, 75
Werner Forman Archive: 3 (bottom), 33 (bottom left and right), 49
Zimbabwe Institute of Vigital Arts: 52

Cover illustration by Julie Paschkis from HEAD, BODY, LEGS © 2002 by Julie Paschkis, text by Won-Ldy Paye and Margaret H. Lippert. Reprinted by permission of Henry Holt and Company, LLC.

Cover illustration by Julie Paschkis from MRS. CHICKEN AND THE HUNGRY CROCODILE © 2003 by Julie Paschkis, text by Won-Ldy Paye and Margaret H. Lippert. Reprinted by permission of Henry Holt and Company, LLC.

Digital Scanning by Superskill Graphics Pte Ltd

Written by
PAUL ROZARIO

Edited by
SELINA KUO

Edited in the U.S. by
CATHERINE GARDNER
ALAN WACHTEL

Designed by
JAILANI BASARI

Picture research by
SUSAN JANE MANUEL

First published in North America in 2003 by
Gareth Stevens Publishing
A World Almanac Education Group Company
330 West Olive Street, Suite 100
Milwaukee, Wisconsin 53212 USA

Please visit our web site at
www.garethstevens.com
For a free color catalog describing
Gareth Stevens Publishing's list of high-quality
books and multimedia programs,
call 1-800-542-2595 (USA) or 1-800-387-3178 (Canada).
Gareth Stevens Publishing's fax: (414) 332-3567.

© **TIMES MEDIA PRIVATE LIMITED 2003**
Originated and designed by
Times Editions
An imprint of Times Media Private Limited
A member of the Times Publishing Group
Times Centre, 1 New Industrial Road
Singapore 536196
http://www.timesone.com.sg/te

Library of Congress Cataloging-in-Publication Data
Rozario, Paul.
Liberia / by Paul Rozario.
p. cm. — (Countries of the world)
Summary: Provides an overview of the
geography, history, government, people, arts, foods,
and other aspects of life in Liberia.
ISBN 0-8368-2366-4 (lib. bdg.)
1. Liberia—Juvenile literature. [1. Liberia.] I. Title.
II. Countries of the world (Milwaukee, Wis.)
DT624.R69   2003
966.62—dc21   2003045560

Printed in Singapore

1 2 3 4 5 6 7 8 9 07 06 05 04 03

Contents

AN OVERVIEW OF LIBERIA

Founded by African Americans, the Republic of Liberia is the oldest republic in Africa. Despite such a historic beginning, Liberia today is struggling to emerge from more than twenty years of violence and civil war. With an abundance of natural resources, such as timber and rubber, Liberia has the potential to develop toward a more stable economy and society. The country is home to some of the last tropical rain forests in West Africa and several endangered species, and Liberia's population is composed of diverse and rich cultures. Since the civil war officially ended in late 1996, Liberians have been rebuilding what they can of their country's political, economic, and social infrastructure.

Opposite: **As violence grew during Liberia's civil war, the Economic Community of West African States responded by sending an armed monitoring group into Liberia to enforce peace.**

Below: **Two children raise the Liberian flag with pride.**

THE FLAG OF LIBERIA

Called the "Lone Star," the Liberian flag has eleven horizontal stripes that alternate between red and white. Red stripes are at the top and bottom of the flag. A blue square is positioned in the top left corner of the flag, and a white, five-pointed star is at the center of the square. The star represents Liberia's status as Africa's first republic, while the eleven stripes represent the original number of signers of the Liberian Declaration of Independence. The colors red, white, and blue respectively represent valor, purity, and fidelity. The flag was adopted on August 24, 1847.

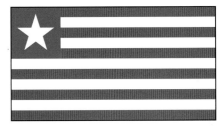

Geography

Liberia is situated in West Africa and occupies a total area of about 43,000 square miles (111,370 square kilometers). The country is bordered by the Republic of Guinea to the north; Côte d'Ivoire, or the Ivory Coast, to the east; the Atlantic Ocean to the south and west; and the Republic of Sierra Leone to the northwest.

Liberia's landscape can be divided into four main regions. The regions are parallel to one another and to the country's coastline, which is about 360 miles (579 kilometers) long.

The Coastal Plains and Rolling Hills

Lying closest to the sea are coastal plains, which span the country's entire coastline. The coastal plains extend inland for varying distances, generally not exceeding 25 miles (40 km). The coastal plains have a variety of geographical features, including sandy beaches, lagoons, mangrove swamps, and savannas. Patches of forest, rubber plantations, and farms

LAKE PISO

Located near the city of Robertsport in Grand Cape Mount County, Lake Piso is Liberia's largest lake. Lake Piso is connected to the Atlantic Ocean via an outlet and is a saltwater lake. The lake is one of Liberia's most famous tourist sites.

Below: Liberia is home to many beautiful beaches, including this one just outside of Monrovia, the country's capital city.

growing cassava, rice, and other crops are also found on the coastal plains. A few rocky outcrops, such as Cape Mount and Cape Palmas, dot the otherwise flat terrain.

Next to the coastal plains, the second region is characterized by lush, green hills that have an average height of about 300 feet (91 meters). Cocoa and coffee plantations thrive on the hilly terrain, alongside dense, tropical rain forests.

The Mountainous North

Liberia's land gradually rises as it extends farther inland. In the third geographical region, low mountains ranging between 600 and 1,000 feet (183 and 305 m) in height are scattered among forests of valuable timber, such as teak, camwood, red ironwood, and mahogany. Savannas are also found at this altitude.

The fourth and most inland region of Liberia is characterized by the country's northern highlands that border Guinea. The highlands consist of the Nimba Range, in Nimba County, and the Wologizi Range, in Lofa County. The two ranges are part of the Guinea Highlands that extend into Sierra Leone, Guinea, and Côte d'Ivoire. Some of Liberia's tallest mountains can be found in the Nimba Range. Part of the Wologizi Range, Mount Wuteve, or Wutivi, is Liberia's highest peak, at 4,528 feet (1,380 m).

ABUNDANT WATER RESOURCES

Liberia's major rivers are the Mano, Morro, and Cavalla rivers. The Mano and Morro rivers form part of the northern border with Sierra Leone, while the Cavalla River forms a section of the frontier between Liberia and Côte d'Ivoire. Other rivers include the Loffa, St. Paul, St. John, and Cess, or Cestos, rivers. Many of the country's rivers have their sources in the highlands of Côte d'Ivoire or Guinea.

Liberia's rivers tend to flow perpendicular to the country's coastline. In some areas, the rivers can become difficult to navigate because of rapids, waterfalls, rocks, and sandbanks. Some rivers, such as the St. Paul, have been used to produce hydroelectric power. The hydroelectric dam at St. Paul, however, was destroyed during the country's civil war.

Climate

Altitude is the main cause of temperature variations in Liberia. The climate along the country's low-lying coastal plains is warm and humid throughout the year, while the inland regions tend to be cooler and drier. The coolest average temperatures are recorded in the country's northern highlands, where the average annual temperature is 65° Fahrenheit (18° Celsius). By the coast, the average temperature is 80° F (27° C), but the tropical heat is moderated by frequent sea breezes.

Liberia experiences a dry season from November to April and a rainy season from May to October. Grand Cape Mount County, where as much as 205 inches (5,207 millimeters) of rain has been known to fall, receives the most precipitation in the country. Less rain is received in the country's inland regions, where averages of about 70 inches (1,778 mm) are recorded each year. During the rainy season, the average humidity along the coastal plains reaches about 82 percent.

Between December and March, Liberia experiences the harmattan winds, which originate in the Sahara Desert in North Africa. Blowing across many countries in West Africa, these winds carry a haze of fine dust particles that cover everything in their path. The harmattan winds usually reach Liberia's coastal plains in December, when they cool temperatures and reduce humidity from 78 percent to about 50 percent.

Left: **Traveling during the rainy season can be difficult because rivers often overflow and flood roads. The country's inland regions are particularly vulnerable to floods during the country's rainy season.**

Left: Liberia's forests are home to antelopes, lemurs, porcupines, chimpanzees, and colobus monkeys. Anteaters, mongooses, and several species of poisonous snakes also roam the forests.

BIRDS OF LIBERIA

Bird life in Liberia is rich. Liberian forests support a large variety of rarely seen birds, including the lesser kestrel and the indigenous Liberia Greenbul. These and other bird species are being threatened by changes in their habitat. *(A Closer Look, page 46)*

THE RIVER HORSE

The hippopotamus is also known as the river horse. In Liberia, the pygmy hippopotamus is a threatened species. *(A Closer Look, page 66)*

LOGGING AND THE ENVIRONMENT

Few sources agree on how much of Liberia is covered in forests, with estimates ranging from 18 to 47 percent of the country. Liberian rain forests, however, form the longest continuous section of the Upper Guinea Forest, which is a region of moist, tropical rain forests that spans the West African coast, from Guinea to Togo. *(A Closer Look, page 60)*

Plants and Animals

Liberia's forests are famous for their rich biodiversity and boast more than 235 types of trees. Teak, mahogany, and ebony trees are valuable because of the timber they provide. Trees such as kola and cotton trees are valuable because of the crops that they bear. In Liberia, two types of rubber trees exist — the indigenous *Funtumia elastica* and the imported *Hevea brasiliensis*. The latter variety is the basis of Liberia's commercial rubber industry.

The white-shouldered duiker and the zebra antelope are indigenous animals in Liberia. The country's rivers are home to crocodiles, pygmy hippopotamuses, and several varieties of fish. Liberia's coastal waters and mangrove swamps support endangered West African manatees and sea turtles. Liberia once had abundant animal life, but many kinds of animals, including elephants, buffaloes, and leopards, are disappearing. About eighteen of the country's mammal species and of its ten bird species are threatened or endangered. One national park and several nature reserves have been set up to conserve Liberia's biodiversity, and conservation plans have been drawn up by local and international environmental agencies to help preserve Liberia's rich natural environment.

History

Early History

The land that is Liberia today was once the home of Mande, Kru, and other African peoples who spoke similar languages. These peoples are believed to have migrated from Sudan, first arriving in the twelfth century. Also known as the Guinea Coast cultures, these peoples initially survived by a mixture of hunting and farming. By the mid-thirteenth century, the Guinea Coast peoples were trading slaves, gold, and kola nuts with the northern savanna kingdoms of Mali and Songhay.

The First Europeans

In 1461, Pedro de Sintra, a Portuguese sailor, reached the coast of Liberia. He is believed to be the first European to make contact with the Guinea Coast cultures. Present-day Liberia and its surrounding areas later became famous as the place where European traders searched for a spice called Melegueta pepper. Melegueta pepper was known to many as the "Grains of Paradise," and the region became known as the Grain Coast. Gradually, other commodities, such as gold, palm oil, and slaves, also were traded with the Europeans. From the 1600s to the early 1800s, the transatlantic slave trade was the dominant commercial activity along the West African coast.

Opposite: **A young Liberian girl touches the monument that depicts Liberia's beginning as a colony for African-Americans.**

Left: **This is an artist's impression of an early European settlement in the region that is now Liberia.**

The American Colonization Society

By the early 1800s, there were many free blacks in the United States. They were either freed slaves or freeborn descendants of former slaves. In 1816, the American Colonization Society (ACS) was founded to settle freed and freeborn African Americans in Africa. The supporters of ACS had a wide variety of motivations. Many white Americans felt that freed slaves and whites should not live together in the same society, fearing that the presence of freed slaves could incite rebellion in the slaves still held in bondage in the southern states. Others promoted the colonization of Africa by black Americans in order to help spread Christianity. Some believed that resettlement would allow blacks to live free of racial discrimination. Yet others thought colonization would hasten the demise of slavery in the United States.

By the early 1820s, ACS established a colony — Liberia — on the Grain Coast of West Africa. Other groups, including the New York City Colonization Society and the Maryland Colonization Society, soon followed suit. Most of these early colonies later combined to form the Republic of Liberia in 1847, with Joseph Jenkins Roberts as the republic's first president.

THE AMERICAN COLONIZATION SOCIETY

Founded in 1816, the American Colonization Society was responsible for sending more than twelve thousand African Americans to Liberia. The society was officially dissolved only in 1964.
(A Closer Look, page 44)

JOSEPH JENKINS ROBERTS

Joseph Roberts was Liberia's first president. Originally a wealthy trader from Virginia, Roberts emigrated to Liberia in 1829.
(A Closer Look, page 54)

A Divided Society

From the start, Liberia's first immigrants from the United States, called Americo-Liberians, sought to distinguish themselves from indigenous Liberians. In fact, Liberia's first constitution did not explicitly extend equal rights to the indigenous peoples. The jurisdiction of the constitution was also limited mainly to the coastal areas, which could be more closely watched by the government from the capital in Monrovia. Americo-Liberians and indigenous Liberians, particularly the Kru and Grebo tribes, had occasional skirmishes, which escalated in 1822, 1856, and 1875. Indigenous Liberians were resentful that the government taxed them and, in some instances, forced them to perform labor in conditions that resembled slavery. Americo-Liberians, on the other hand, were afraid that granting more rights to the indigenous peoples, who formed a vast majority of the population, would reduce their own political power.

Into the Twentieth Century

Americo-Liberians, although only a tiny fraction of the Liberian population, dominated the country into the twentieth century. Reforms to bring indigenous Liberians into the national life of the country were implemented slowly. Citizenship was eventually granted to all of Liberia's inhabitants, and some

Left: This illustration is an artist's impression of the mutiny aboard *Amistad,* a slave ship, in 1839. Although first captured by U.S. naval forces, the slaves were later set free by the U.S. Supreme Court. Most of them were captured from either Sierra Leone or Liberia. Apart from Americo- and indigenous Liberians, Liberia's early population also included freed slaves from the Caribbean and South America, as well as those who had been rescued from illegal slave ships.

Left: In 1996, when the civil war was drawing to a close, Krahn fighters stormed the streets of Monrovia to continue their war efforts. Throughout the 1980s, leader Samuel Doe's time in power was fraught with many attempted coups and much social unrest, which were partly caused by Doe's bias in favor of his own Krahn people. Members of other ethnic groups, including the Dan and Mano, resented his favoritism.

indigenous groups came to be represented in government, although a few uprisings against the authorities occurred during the 1910s and 1930s. In 1944, William Tubman became president and began a series of successful reforms aimed at developing the economy and closing the wide social and economic gaps that separated Americo- and indigenous Liberians.

The 1970s and 1980s

William Tolbert succeeded William Tubman as president. Under Tolbert, Liberia entered a period of economic decline triggered by falls in world demand for rubber and iron ore, the country's main exports. The Liberian people's dissatisfaction with the government brewed and exploded into bloody riots in 1979. In 1980, Tolbert was killed in a violent coup led by Master Sergeant Samuel Kanyon Doe. Doe later won the presidential elections held in 1985 and became Liberia's first non-Americo-Liberian president. Doe's regime, however, deepened the economic and social divisions between the ruling group and ordinary Liberians. In December 1989, a rebellion began in Nimba County that eventually engulfed Liberia in an all-out civil war.

WILLIAM TUBMAN

William Tubman was Liberia's president from 1944 to 1971. Under Tubman, Liberia gained considerable economic and social stability.
(A Closer Look, page 72)

LIBERIA DURING WORLD WAR II

Liberia was a strategic partner of the Allied forces during World War II. Liberia produced vast quantities of rubber at a time when the Japanese occupation of Southeast Asia stopped rubber supplies traditionally provided by that part of the world.

The Civil War (1989–1996)

Charles Ghankay Taylor, who had previously worked in the Doe government, headed the rebellion. His force, the National Patriotic Front of Liberia (NPFL), fought heavy battles with the Armed Forces of Liberia (AFL). While the government forces were mainly made up of Krahn fighters, the Dan and Mano peoples supported the NPFL. Both parties committed terrible atrocities against civilians, prompting peacekeeping military action from neighboring countries. Doe was killed by rebels in 1990. In the years that followed, fighting raged between the NPFL, the AFL, and other factions, including the Independent National Patriotic Front of Liberia (INPFL) and the United Liberation Movement of Liberia for Democracy (ULIMO).

A Fragile Peace

In late 1996, Liberia's main factions approved a peace plan, and the fighting ceased. Charles Taylor won the presidential election held in July 1997. ECOWAS then launched a program to disarm the various military factions. In 2002, Liberia still laid in ruins, although some steps had been taken to rebuild the country's infrastructure and return refugees to their homes. Ethnic tensions have persisted. Between the late 1990s and early 2000s, clashes between the Loma, Mandingo, Mano, and Dan peoples were reported in Nimba, Bong, and Lofa counties.

ECOWAS

The Economic Community of West African States (ECOWAS) is a regional organization of West African states that includes Liberia as a member. ECOWAS intervened in Liberia's civil war on several occasions but met with limited success. ECOWAS sent troops to Liberia to enforce peace when the civil war first broke out. The military force of ECOWAS was known as ECOMOG, or the ECOWAS Monitoring Group. ECOWAS also helped set up a transitional government in Monrovia, but they were ineffective in the countryside, where the NPFL dominated.

RENEWED UNREST

In late 2000, a new conflict arose in Lofa County, where one faction, called Liberians United for Reconciliation and Democracy (LURD), launched a campaign to topple Charles Taylor and his administration. By mid-2002, LURD had advanced toward Monrovia but were driven back by government forces. Today, there are fears that the LURD movement will further destabilize Liberia and West Africa as a whole.

Left: On August 10, 1992, these NPFL soldiers in Tapeta stood at attention outside their camp.

Alexander Peal (1945–)

Alexander Peal studied forestry and wildlife management in his youth. Also a talented soccer player, Peal joined the national soccer team as a goalkeeper. He became a soccer celebrity in Liberia, and his fame helped to promote his conservation work. In the 1970s, he joined the Liberian Bureau of Forestry and Wildlife Conservation and later helped to establish Liberia's only national park. In 1986, Peal cofounded the Society for the Conservation of Nature of Liberia, which is Liberia's first non-governmental organization dedicated to preserving the country's environment. For his environmental work, Peal has won several international awards, including the 2000 Goldman Environmental Prize and the 2001 Whitley Gold Award.

Alexander Peal

Samuel Kanyon Doe (c.1950–1990)

Originally from Grand Gedeh County, Samuel Doe joined the army when he was eighteen years old. After many years of service, Doe was promoted to the rank of master sergeant in 1979. Like many indigenous Liberians, Doe was unhappy with the rule of the True Whig Party, which was dominated by Americo-Liberians. Doe plotted with Krahn soldiers to topple the government and, in 1980, they attacked the Executive Mansion in Monrovia. Doe then ruled Liberia for nearly ten years, first as chairman of the People's Redemption Council and later as president of the country. Killed at the outbreak of the civil war, Doe's time in power was corrupt and brutal.

Charles Taylor

Charles Ghankay Taylor (1948–)

Son of a Liberian judge, Charles Taylor pursued a degree in economics at Bentley College in Waltham, Massachusetts, in the 1970s. He later served as the director of Liberia's General Services Administration under President Samuel Doe. In 1984, Taylor was accused of corruption and fled to the United States. Taylor eventually returned to Liberia, where he formed the National Patriotic Front of Liberia (NPFL), a militia group that launched a rebellion against the Liberian government in late 1989. The rebellion plunged the country into a bloody civil war that lasted until late 1996. In mid-1997, elections were held, and Charles Taylor became president of Liberia.

Government and the Economy

Historically, Liberian government had been dominated by the True Whig Party, which ruled from 1878 to 1980. Because the party was formed by Americo-Liberians, it tended to overlook the needs of the indigenous Liberian population. The True Whig Party eventually collapsed under the combined pressure of an impoverished economy and disenchanted Liberians. Since 1980, when Master Sergeant Samuel Doe came to power, Liberia has been run by military men whose governments have been composed of members of the rival political parties that played significant parts in the 1989 civil war. Officially, however, Liberia has had a civilian government since 1997.

Above: **The national emblem of Liberia was inspired by that of the United States.**

The Constitution of 1986

The Liberian constitution is modeled after that of the United States. In effect since 1986, Liberia's consitution was first drafted in 1984 and is the second in the country's history. The first was drawn up in 1847, when Liberia became an independent republic.

POLITICAL PARTIES

The 1984 constitution allows different political parties to participate in elections. Today, Liberia has many political parties, including the ruling National Patriotic Party, the Unity Party, and the All Liberia Coalition Party. Political activity, nevertheless, has been less than vigorous, partly because of the government's attempts to stifle opposition to its policies.

Left: **A woman casts her vote in the 1997 presidential elections at a rural polling station near Gbarnga in Bong County.**

Liberia's constitution provides for three branches of government: legislative, executive, and judiciary. The legislative branch divides into the House of Representatives (sixty-four members) and the Senate (twenty-six members). Members of the House of Representatives are elected to serve six-year terms and members of the Senate to serve nine-year terms. The executive branch is led by the president, who is elected to serve a six-year term. Ministers of the cabinet are appointed by the president and are subject to the approval of the Senate. The judiciary consists of a Supreme Court, which is the country's highest court, and a system of surbordinate courts. The president appoints the chief justice, the country's top judge, who leads the judiciary.

Above: **In 1998, two young Liberians stood outside the former Ministry of Internal Affairs that was being used as a shelter for Liberians displaced by the civil war. Many of Liberia's institutions, including the judiciary, did not always function during the civil war. Today, Liberia is rebuilding its infrastructure with the help of foreign aid.**

Local Government

Liberia is divided into fifteen counties, and each county is led by a superintendent appointed by the president. Other local officials include district commissioners, mayors, and councillors in the cities, and paramount, clan, and town chiefs in rural or more traditional communities.

Economy

Agriculture, the main economic activity in Liberia, came to a standstill in the 1990s because many farmers were killed, forced off their lands, or made to join military factions. Despite some improvement, food production in Liberia today has yet to return to the levels achieved before the civil war. Liberian farmers mainly produce rice, cocoa, coffee, palm oil, sugar cane, and cassava. In 2000, the agricultural sector employed about 70 percent of the Liberian workforce.

Industrial output of rubber, a major Liberian export, also fell dramatically during the civil war. Although rubber production has increased since 1997, output levels are still far below what they were before the war began. Reasons for the rubber industry's slow recovery include a lack of investment and a weak, postwar global market for rubber.

Liberia's mining industry has traditionally focused on iron ore. The iron ore industry, however, underwent serious decline not only because of the civil war, but also because of a depletion of the country's iron ore reserves. Today, the Liberian mining industry has turned its focus to gold and diamonds.

MINING

Liberia was one of the world's top producers of iron ore in the 1960s and 1970s. Large deposits of iron ore were discovered in the Bomi and Mano hills and in the Bong and Nimba ranges.
(*A Closer Look, page 62*)

RUBBER

In 1926, Harvey Firestone, an American, established Liberia's first large-scale rubber plantation. Since then, rubber has become an important export.
(*A Closer Look, page 68*)

DIAMONDS: A CONTROVERSIAL RESOURCE

Liberia has significant deposits of diamonds that are far from fully exploited. Liberia's diamond industry, however, has been controversially linked to the war in Sierra Leone.
(*A Closer Look, page 50*)

Left: A palm tree stands in the middle of a newly cultivated vegetable farm.

Transportation

Liberia has about 6,583 miles (10,600 km) of roads, but only an estimated 408 miles (657 km) are paved. A major road links Monrovia to Freetown in Sierra Leone, while another links Monrovia to Gahnpa (Ganta), in Nimba County. Liberian roads are generally in poor condition and in need of repairs.

A rail network was built to support the country's once-thriving iron ore industry. One set of tracks linked Monrovia to mines in Bong and Lofa, while another was laid between Buchanan and Yekepa. With the closure of the country's main iron ore mines, however, there has been no traffic on Liberia's railway.

Liberia has ports at Monrovia, Buchanan, Greenville, and Harper. Shipping services were disrupted during the civil war and port facilities were damaged. Some efforts have since been made to repair the country's port facilities.

Liberia's international airports are the Robertsfield International Airport in Harbel and the James Spriggs Payne Airport in Monrovia.

Above: Merkur River, **a cargo ship from Monrovia, docks at the Port of Savannah in Georgia. In 2000, Liberian exports were mainly sold to the United States, Belgium, Germany, and Italy.**

People and Lifestyle

A Diverse Heritage

In 2002, Liberia's population was estimated to be approaching 3.3 million. Indigenous Africans belonging to a wide variety of ethnic groups make up about 95 percent of the Liberian population. The larger indigenous groups include the Kpelle, Bassa, Gio, Kru, Grebo, Mano, Krahn, Gola, Gbandi, Loma, Kissi, Vai, and Bella. Liberia has suffered ethnic tensions in the past, but many Liberians today feel the need to focus on national unity and less on ethnic divisions.

Of the remaining 5 percent, about half are Americo-Liberians and the other half are Congo People, or descendants of immigrants from the Caribbean. Similar to the Americo-Liberians, these Caribbean immigrants were also freed slaves. Small communities of non-Africans, including Lebanese, live in some cities.

Below, left: Liberian women give birth to an average of six children each. The country has a relatively young population. In 2002, about 43 percent of Liberians were under the age of fourteen.

Below, right: Women in Liberia tend to outlive men, with women living for an average of fifty-three years, while men live an average of fifty years. Only about 3.5 percent of Liberians reach age sixty-five or older.

Urban and Rural Life

Throughout Liberia's history, its countryside has been neglected by its government in Monrovia. As a result, Liberia has gradually divided into modern, urban areas and traditional, rural regions. While the civil war disrupted everyday life in both the cities and the countryside, the rural regions are taking longer to recover from the devastation.

About 40 percent of all Liberians live in the major urban areas of Monrovia, Buchanan, Harper, and Greenville. Inland, many populate the smaller cities of Gbarnga, Tchien (Zwedru), Harbel, Sanniquellie, Voinjama, and Gahnpa. Liberians living in the cities are generally more Westernized in their attitudes and outlook. City folk, for example, usually practice monogamy, while men in rural Liberia may follow traditional practices and have more than one wife. Most rural Liberians are farmers, with a small number of traders, artists, and hunters among them. Urban dwellers work in a variety of fields, including industry. Perhaps the biggest difference between city life and village life in Liberia is the architecture and landscape: Liberia's cities, large and small, have tall buildings and houses built with cement and other permanent materials. Villages, on the other hand, are dominated by thatch-roof huts and simple, wooden structures.

MONROVIA

Liberia's capital city, Monrovia, suffered extensive damage during the civil war. Today, the capital is in the process of being rebuilt, albeit slowly.

(*A Closer Look,* page 64)

Family and Social Ties

Family ties are very important to Liberians. Relations are close between members of extended families, and it is common to see several generations of one family living either in the same house or near each other. The elderly are respected in Liberian society. In villages, elderly Liberians often serve as local leaders and judges, to whom people can turn for help in solving problems.

In some indigenous cultures, social institutions, such as the *Poro* (POH-roh), for men, and the *Sande* (SAHN-day), for women, help people strengthen social bonds and keep up traditional ways and knowledge. The Sande and Poro are societies that teach their members customary law, traditional religion, and proper ways of behaving. Described by some anthropologists as secret societies, these social organizations also help teach practical skills, such as how to construct bridges and heal with herbs. The civil war disrupted the work of these social institutions, but they are now enjoying a revival in areas of the countryside recovering from the war.

Below: In 1998, this Liberian family in the Buduburam Refugee Camp in Ghana was in the process of being forcibly sent back to Liberia. By mid-2002, more than 400,000 Liberians had been displaced by the civil war. This number included Liberian refugees in Sierra Leone, Côte d'Ivoire, Guinea, Nigeria, and Ghana, as well as some 200,000 Liberians who had been displaced within Liberia itself.

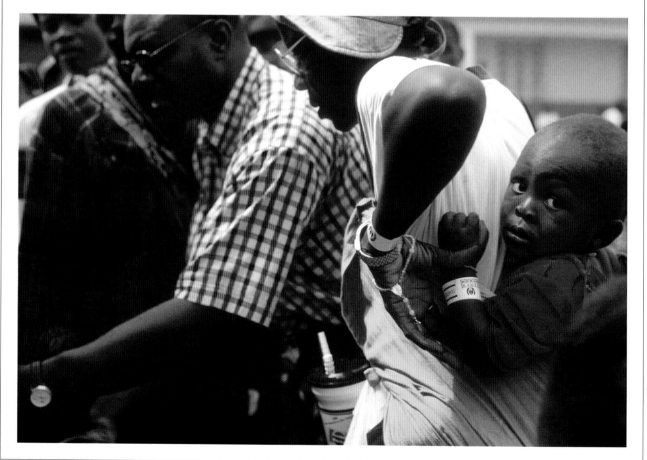

Women in Liberia

Although women hold important positions in Liberian society and work in all sectors of the Liberian economy, they are faced with many challenges. Before the civil war, women held about one quarter of all professional and technical jobs in Monrovia. The status of women suffered, however, during the civil war, when many became the victims of rape and violence. The government has since made efforts to raise the status of women by implementing a series of programs aimed at reducing poverty, increasing literacy, and developing skills. Community-based organizations, such as the Liberian Women's Initiative, the Liberia Rural Women's Association, and the Association for Female Lawyers, are also active in promoting women's interests.

Women's groups in Liberia are particularly concerned about the rights of women under traditional Liberian law. Most Liberian women marry under traditional law, under which they are not entitled to custody of their children or to inherit property from their husbands if their husbands die. Women's groups in Liberia have been lobbying for equal rights for women married under traditional law and women married under civil law.

Above: **Couples in Liberia can marry according to either traditional law or civil law. Under traditional law, a man is allowed to have more than one wife. Under civil law, he is only allowed to have one. Most marriages in Liberia follow traditional law. Polygyny, or the practice of having more than one wife, however, is more common in rural than in urban areas.**

Elementary School and High School

Officially, education is compulsory for Liberian children between the ages of seven and fifteen and is free in public schools. Elementary school spans six years and is followed by six years of high school. Some Liberian children attend nursery school and kindergarten before they start elementary school.

Secondary education is divided into three years of junior high school (grades seven through nine) and three years of senior high school (grades ten through twelve). Students in the ninth-grade have to pass an examination administered by the West African Examination Council before proceeding to senior high school. Students who successfully complete senior high school are awarded the West African Examination Council Certificate, which permits them to enter a university.

Rebuilding the Education System

Liberia's education system has suffered serious setbacks because of the civil war. Most of the country's schools, including colleges and universities, were destroyed during the war. Liberian students generally had little or no access to educational services for nearly a decade.

Lack of educational opportunity is a major problem facing Liberian refugees in countries such as Sierra Leone and Guinea. In Guinea, for example, organizations such as the United Nations Educational, Scientific, and Cultural Organization (UNESCO) and the International Rescue Committee (IRC) support refugee schools that educate Liberian children at preschool, primary, and secondary levels. The refugee schools teach the Liberian curriculum and arrange for students to sit for examinations that will help them enter Liberian schools once they return to Liberia.

Left: School enrollment rates increased significantly in 1999, but despite the government's efforts, estimates in 2002 suggested that only 40 percent of Liberian children actually attended school.

In 1999, the government announced that nearly 11 percent of the national budget would be spent on education, and it began a program of intensive reconstruction that increased the number of primary schools in Liberia from 1,500 to more than 4,500. Under the same program, the number of secondary schools in Liberia rose to 461, an increase of over 90 percent from the previous year. Most of these schools, however, have been built in and around Monrovia and do not benefit students in the countryside.

Higher Education

Liberia has seven institutions of higher learning — the University of Liberia, Cuttington University College, the William V. S. Tubman College of Technology, Don Bosco Polytechnic, A. M. E. University, A. M. E. Zion University College, and the United Methodist University. Although independent, these institutions receive financial assistance from the government. The Liberian education system also includes vocational schools, which provide education in industry, agriculture, and other technical areas. Most Liberian institutions of post-secondary education closed during the civil war because many of them suffered physical damage to their classrooms and laboratories. Today, these institutions are relying on donations from international organizations to rebuild their facilities and resume classes.

A SHORTAGE OF TEACHERS

Problems saddling the Liberian educational system include shortages of trained teachers, textbooks, and school supplies. Before the civil war, the Liberian educational system was supported by about 12,000 qualified teachers. Only about 3,000 teachers remained in the country in 1999, according to figures from a relief organization.

Religion

The Constitution of Liberia guarantees freedom of religion. About 40 percent of Liberians are Christian and about 20 percent are Muslim. The remaining 40 percent of Liberians follow traditional indigenous religions. These estimates, however, vary from source to source because many Muslim and Christian Liberians combine their religious beliefs with some traditional indigenous practices. Christianity has always been more prominent in Liberia, and the government has tended to favor the religion in public life. Many public ceremonies open and close with Christian prayers and hymns. Churches run many schools, clinics, and welfare programs in the country.

Islam in Liberia

Islam is common among the various Mande peoples of northern and eastern Liberia, as well as among the Vai ethnic group in the northwestern Liberia. Liberian Muslims, like Muslims around the world, worship in mosques. They pray five times a day and fast between sunrise and sundown during the holy month of

Below: Liberians bow their heads during a Christian service at Sacred Heart Cathedral. Christian denominations present in Liberia include the Lutheran, Methodist, Baptist, Presbyterian, and Roman Catholic churches. While some Liberian churches are independent, others are linked to churches overseas. The Providence Baptist Church in Monrovia is Liberia's oldest church.

Ramadan. Their most important holy days are Ramadan and *Eid al-Fitr*, which marks the end of Ramadan.

Above: **Liberians at a Red Cross center for people displaced by the civil war attend prayer services.**

Tensions between Christians and Muslims exist in Liberia. Because the government favors Christian gestures of faith over Islamic ones, Muslims have tended to feel unrecognized, and clashes between the government and Muslim groups have erupted over this issue. Liberian Muslims receive financial help from Islamic organizations in other countries for various projects, including opening schools and running healthcare programs.

Indigenous Religions

Liberians who follow indigenous religions can be found throughout the country. These indigenous religions are deeply animistic. Animists believe that nature and natural objects, such as trees, rocks, and rivers, are full of spirits that have the power to do good or evil. Animists generally also believe in ancestor spirits, and their many worshipping rites involve much singing and dancing. Liberians who practice traditional indigenous religions perform many coming-of-age rites, including rituals for birth, initiation into adulthood, and marriage.

Language and Literature

Liberian English

English is the official language of Liberia and the native language of about one-fifth of all Liberians. The English spoken by ordinary Liberians, however, is quite different from the English used in government and education. A type of Pidgin English, everyday Liberian English has been influenced by both the vocabulary and grammar of indigenous African languages and the way African slaves used to speak English in the southern United States in the 1700s and 1800s. Examples of Liberian Pidgin English are "basiko" for "bicycle," "orinsh" for "orange," and "panapo" for "pineapple." Educated Liberians regard American English as the correct form of English.

A Complex System of Languages

Most Liberians speak several languages, including English. Liberia's indigenous ethnic groups speak more than twenty languages among them, and each language generally belongs to either the Mande, Kwa, or Mel linguistic family. Mande-speakers, the largest group, include the Kpelle, Loma, Vai, and Mano peoples.

THE KPELLE

The Kpelle are the largest indigenous ethnic group in Liberia. Known by the same name, the language they speak is part of the Mande linguistic family.
(*A Closer Look, page 56*)

KWA AND MEL

Most Kwa speakers live in southeastern and eastern Liberia, and they include members of the Bassa, Kru, Grebo, Bella, and Krahn ethnic groups. Mel speakers, including the Gola and the Kissi, are believed to be among the oldest inhabitants of Liberia. They generally live in the country's north and along the country's northwestern coast.

Left: Liberia is the only black African state where English is the native tongue of a significant percentage of the population.

Left: **Bernt Karlsson, a Swedish private collector, has an extensive collection of works on Liberia.**

INDIGENOUS ALPHABETS

A few of Liberia's African languages use unique writing scripts. These include the Vai and Bassa languages. Duala Bukare developed the Vai script in the early nineteenth century, while Dr. Flo Darvin Lewis revived the Bassa script in the early twentieth century.
(A Closer Look, page 52)

Liberian Literature

Charles E. Cooper, a diplomat, wrote the first Liberian novel, *Love in Ebony* (1932), under the pseudonym of Varfelli Karlee. In the book, Cooper tells a love story set against the traditional life of the indigenous peoples who resided in Liberia's inland regions. The book also provides insights into the workings of the Poro in Liberian rural life.

Written by Wilton Sankawulo, *The Rain and the Night* (1979) is another important Liberian novel. Other Liberian literary classics include *Murder in the Cassava Patch* (1963), *The Money Doubler* (1968), *The Mystic Reformation of Gondolia* (1953), and *Monkey Storm* (1977). The first two titles were written by Bai T.J. Moore, while the latter two were written by Roland Tombekai Dempster and E. Toimu-A. Reeves, respectively.

Liberian authors have also written many short stories, which commonly explore the conflict between traditional and modern values. *So say one, so say all and other West African Stories* and *Modern West African Short Stories from Liberia* are two short-story collections that were published in the 1970s.

LIBERIAN FOLKTALES

Much of Liberia's literary heritage is oral in nature. The country has one of the great West African storytelling traditions. In West African cultures, storytelling is a way of preserving and passing down historical and cultural information to the next generation. Storytellers are widely regarded as part singer, part entertainer, and part historian.
(A Closer Look, page 58)

Arts

Art in Daily Life

Liberia's diverse ethnic composition has resulted in a rich artistic tradition that includes music, dance, sculpture, and painting. In the villages in the interior of the country, art is very much part of daily life. Before the civil war, the Sande and Poro were especially active in keeping traditional arts alive. Members learned weaving, woodcarving, basketry, sculpture, music, and dancing. Today, the Sande and Poro continue to play a part, if less active, in helping Liberians preserve their artistic and cultural heritage.

Song and Dance

Singing is so vital to Liberian rural life that it accompanies just about any activity or event, ranging from routine household chores to welcoming guests to major celebrations such as births and weddings. Rural Liberians sing at home, while working in the fields, or when working together on large projects, such as mending fishnets and preparing for village celebrations.

Indigenous Liberians perform a great variety of dances. The Dan, or Gio, people of northern Liberia, in particular, have a special dance that involves a masked dancer and a drummer. During the dance, the two perform precise hand and foot movements while appearing to follow each other within the performance space. Other dances feature performers that line up in a row or form a circle. Not everyone, however, can perform the same dance. Some dances only feature female dancers, while others only male. Children also have their own special dance that is not performed by adults.

Famous Singers and Musicians

Liberians listen to many local and overseas singers and musicians. Some well-known Liberian singers include Miatta Fahnbulleh, Molly Dorley, Anthony Nagbe, and Fatu Gayflor. Liberian singers often perform a mix of indigenous Liberian music, West African music, and Western rock 'n roll. Many famous Liberian artists and musicians, however, left the country because of the civil war. Today, they are scattered in parts of West Africa, Europe, and North America.

Above: **Soprano Dawn Padmore is one of several well-known Liberian singers who left the country during the civil war. Displaced Liberian musicians and singers often continue to promote Liberian and African music in their adopted countries.**

Opposite: Wearing a traditional headdress and white body paint, a young indigenous Liberian dancer poses for a photograph.

Liberian Drums

Drums are an important part of African music and dance. Drummers keep the rhythm and ensure that the singers, dancers, and other musicians perform in unison. Liberia's musical tradition includes a variety of drums, including the *tardegai* (TAR-duh-GUY), or *damma* (DUHM-mah). Shaped like an hourglass, the tardegai has a piece of animal hide stretched over each of its two ends. Pieces of rope, arranged so that they are parallel to each other, are attached to the drum from end to end. A hammer-shaped stick is used to play the tardegai, which is held under the player's arm. Pulling on the ropes changes the volume or the pitch of the sound the drum makes.

Another type of drum is the *djembe* (JEM-bay), or *sankpah* (SUNG-pah), which is made by stretching a piece of animal hide over one end of a hollowed tree trunk. Players of the djembe use their hands to beat the hide to produce rhythms. The *dun dun* (DOON doon), or *djun djun* (JOON joon), is a type of bass drum. Made by covering each end of a hollowed tree trunks with a piece of hide, it is played with sticks. The *kono* (KOH-noh) drum is unique because it is made entirely of wood. The kono has a two-inch slit cut into it lengthwise and is played using two sticks.

TRADITIONAL MUSICAL INSTRUMENTS

Apart from drums, traditional musical instruments in Liberia include the *balafon* (BAH-luh-fawn), which is a type of xylophone, and the *zaza* (ZAH-zah), which is a shaker made by attaching a mesh of beads to a calabash, or dried gourd. The *kora* (CORE-rah) is a stringed instrument that is popular in West Africa, including in Liberia. The kora consists of twenty-one strings attached to a calabash, and music is produced by strumming and plucking the strings in a way similar to the way a guitar is played.

Colorful Masks and Other Carvings

Liberians dancers sometimes wear colorful and intricately carved wooden masks in their performances. One of the most famous examples of African art in the world, these masks sell for large amounts of money in Western countries. For some Liberians, the masks are not just artistic works, but also channels connecting the spirit and human worlds. These Liberians believe that dancers wearing the masks become the spirits or characters the masks represent. While some masks are worn during religious ceremonies, others are hung up on walls to ward off evil. Fur, animal teeth, and shells are often used to decorate such masks.

Liberian artists produce some of West Africa's most beautiful stone and wood carvings. Animals, mythical beasts, and human figures and heads are common subjects of Liberian sculptures. The Bassa and Dan peoples are famous for making fine wooden carvings of humanlike gods or human figures that are usually modeled after ancestors or other people held in similarly high regard. Sculptures by the Bassa and Dan characteristically have lifelike facial features and incorporate a remarkable amount of detail, including tattoos, beads, and jewelry. The Kissi are better known for carving figures out of soapstone, which is a relatively soft mixture of talc and rock-forming minerals.

DAN MASKS

The Dan, or Gio, people of northern Liberia are famous for the masks they use during their rituals and celebrations.
(*A Closer Look, page 48*)

VAI ARTS

The Vai people of northwestern Liberia have a rich tradition in the performing arts.
(*A Closer Look, page 70*)

Left: Many masks and other wooden carvings produced by the Dan people have become parts of collections of African art at museums and private art galleries around the world.

Leisure and Festivals

How Liberians Relax

Liberians have suffered greatly as a result of the civil war, and it will take a long time for them to recover from the war's devastating effects on so many aspects of Liberian society. Many Liberians today have to work extremely hard in order to earn enough money for themselves and their families. Thus, finding time or money to relax and pursue leisure activities is not a priority for a majority of the population. Few Liberians take overseas vacations or have the money to buy sports equipment. This does not mean, however, that Liberians in general do not enjoy life or take time to relax with friends and family. Liberians enjoy spending time with their families at gatherings for important festivals and celebrations, during which they indulge in much singing and dancing. Playing soccer and board games are also popular and inexpensive forms of recreation.

Left: A fisherman belonging to the Kru ethnic group moves his boat along the beach in Greenville in Singe County.

Left: **Rural Liberian children entertain themselves by playing a ball game.**

Urban and Rural Pastimes

Rural Liberians spend their leisure time somewhat differently than their urban counterparts. City dwellers may go to nightclubs or bars to dance and listen to music, while rural Liberians enjoy dance performances in their village squares. Liberians who live in cities may go to sports stadiums for soccer matches, while those in rural areas play soccer in open fields or spaces. Telling stories is also a popular pastime in Liberian villages. Expert Liberian storytellers can capture their audiences for many hours with traditional folktales and epics. Watching television and listening to the radio are pastimes that are available only to Liberians who can afford to buy radios and televisions. Urban Liberians are also more likely to watch television and listen to the radio because they are more likely to have access to electricity.

Visiting markets to buy food, socialize with friends, and catch up with the latest gossip is something that all Liberians do regardless of where they live. Another popular meeting place is the cookshop. Cookshops, which are small stalls that sell inexpensive meals and snacks, can be found in rural and urban areas throughout Liberia.

TRADITIONAL GAMES

Mancala (mahn-KAH-lah) is a popular traditional game in Liberia. Some Liberians call the game *kboo* (POOH). A popular game across Africa, it is played on a wooden board that has had holes carved into it. Two players place a number of seeds or stones in each of the holes. Relying on mathematical skills and strategies, each player tries to win as many of the opponent's seeds or stones as possible.

Soccer

Soccer is probably the most popular sport in Liberia. Many young Liberians play it for fun, and numerous soccer teams from all over the country play it as a competitive sport. Soccer is also a favorite spectator sport in Liberia. Large crowds often fill the country's stadiums to watch soccer matches.

Liberia has a national organization that monitors and aids the development of soccer in the country. Founded in 1936, the Liberia Football Association organizes Liberia's soccer teams into four divisions. The first division consists of the nation's best teams, including the Mighty Barolle, the Invincible Eleven, and the L.P.R.C. Oilers. Liberia's soccer teams compete against each other to win National League Championship. The nation's highest soccer award, the Barclay Shield, is given to the team that wins this event.

Liberia's national soccer team, the Lone Star, represents the country at international competitions, such as the African Nations Cup and the World Cup. Although the Lone Star has yet to qualify for the World Cup soccer competition, the team came close in 2002, when the Liberians narrowly lost a place to the Nigerians. In the 2002 African Nations Cup competition, the Lone Star team emerged as the one of the top teams in the qualifying rounds but failed to advance to the quarterfinal rounds.

SPORTS BUREAU

Part of the Ministry of Youth and Sports, the Bureau of Sports aims to develop sports on a national level in Liberia. The bureau oversees sporting events held in the country and monitors Liberian sporting associations. The bureau also trains coaches and sports administrators.

Left: A soccer team from Jalay's Town travels to nearby Juazohn for a match. Liberia's soccer clubs take part in regional competitions, including the African Cup Winner's Cup, the *Confédération Africaine de Football* (CAF) Cup, and the African Champion's League.

Left: On December 17, 2001, FIFA president Joseph Blatter (*center*) and Liberian soccer star George Weah (*right*) presented Luis Figo (*left*) of Spanish soccer team Real Madrid with the 2001 FIFA World Player of the Year award.

Liberian Soccer Players Around the World

Many Liberian soccer players join teams outside of the country. Prince Daye, for example, has played for the French soccer team Bastia and is currently playing for a Tunisian soccer team. Liberians currently playing for European clubs include Dulee Johnson and George Gebro. Gebro plays for a Greek team, while Johnson plays for Swedish team BK Hacken. Zizi Roberts plays for the Colorado Rapids, a U.S. team. In Asia, Anthony Ballah plays for Indonesian team Persita Tangarang; Josiah J.B. Seton plays for the Sabah Rhinos, a Malaysian team; and Joseph Amoah and Moses Nyewon play for teams in Thailand.

George Weah is probably Liberia's most famous soccer player. In 1995, Weah's outstanding performance earned him several coveted awards, including the Federation Internationale Football Association (FIFA) World Player of the Year Award, the European Player of the Year Award, and the African Player of the Year Award. Weah also made history by being the first African to be named FIFA World Player of the Year. During his illustrious soccer career, Weah has played for top European teams, such as Italy's AC Milan and France's Paris St. Germain.

OTHER SPORTS IN LIBERIA

Basketball is also popular in Liberia. The Liberian Basketball Federation oversees the game in the country. Basketball teams, such as the Don Bosco Legends and the NPA Pythons, are divided into leagues, and they compete in league championships each year.

Liberia also has sporting associations for volleyball, baseball, tae kwon do, karate, golf, tennis, and track and field. Although the various associations seek to promote their respective sports throughout Liberia, they tend to be more active in Monrovia than anywhere else in the country.

Christian Festivals

Christian Liberians, especially those descended from Americo-Liberians, celebrate Christmas by attending church services either on Christmas Eve or Christmas Day, before sharing in a family meal. Dishes such as roast turkey, ham, and pudding are usually served. Christian Liberians of indigenous African background also go to church before gathering for a family meal. Their church celebrations have a more African flavor and include drumming and dancing. In rural villages, Christmas celebrations are held in the open and involve much singing and dancing. Although most Liberians celebrate Christmas by going to church, they do not give gifts and have Christmas trees.

Other holidays Christian Liberians observe include Good Friday and Easter in March or April, Thanksgiving in early November, and National Fast and Pray Day in April.

Major Muslim Festivals

Muslim Liberians celebrate *Eid al-Fitr* and *Tabaski* (TAH-BAH-skee), which is also known as *Eid al-Adha*. Neither festival is a public holiday in Liberia. Eid al-Fitr markes the end of Ramadan, which is a month of fasting for all Muslims. During Ramadan, Muslims do not eat or drink between sunrise and sundown.

Left: Liberians fill the Sacred Heart Church in Monrovia to attend Palm Sunday Mass.

Muslim Liberians celebrate Tabaski by slaughtering a ram or sheep. The festival celebrates the story of Abraham in the Qur'an and how he obeyed God in all things. Muslim Liberians begin preparing for Tabaski months in advance and make sure they have new clothes and plenty of food for the occasion. During Tabaski, families attend prayer services at mosques before visiting extended family members and friends.

Traditional African Celebrations

Traditional African festivals are held in Liberia to celebrate births, weddings, and rites of passage. These traditional African celebrations are more common in the villages than in the cities. City people do celebrate them, but less elaborately.

Rites of passage mark the initiation of children into adulthood. Because these ceremonial celebrations span over many months, they are only held once every few years. Special huts are built for the celebrations, and the whole community is involved in these events. Older villagers usually teach the youths what is needed in order that they become recognized as adults by the rest of the community. After the ceremonies, the community welcomes its newly initiated members with feasting and dancing.

Above: **Every year, Liberians celebrate a host of secular holidays, which include the birthdays of former presidents Joseph Jenkins Roberts (March 15) and William Tubman (November 29), Unification and Integration Day (May 14), Independence Day (July 26), and Flag Day (August 24). Flag Day commemorates the day in 1847 on which the Liberian national flag was adopted.**

Food

Liberians love spicy food, and they often flavor their food with ingredients such as black pepper, ginger, and small, red peppers. Cayenne pepper, in particular, is favored by Liberians who want to give their meals a fiery taste.

Rice and Cassava

The main staple food in Liberia is rice, which is typically searved rice at lunch and dinner. Liberians eat both locally grown and imported rice. They call imported rice *pusava* (poo-SAH-vah). Rice is usually eaten as part of dishes made either entirely from vegetables or from a combination of vegetables with meat or fish. Different types of stews and sauces are also eaten with rice. One famous rice dish is *jollof* (JAW-lof), a dish also eaten in other parts of West Africa. Jollof is usually made from rice, tomatoes, and chicken. In Liberia, pig's feet, ham, and bacon are sometimes also added to jollof.

A LIBERIAN MEAL

A Liberian meal prepared for a special occasion will consist of dozens of meat, vegetable, fruit, stew, soup, and dessert dishes. All the dishes are brought to the table at once, and diners simply take a little food from each dish. Palm wine and ginger beer are traditional drinks that accompany Liberian meals.

Below: **A man in Singe County eats a breakfast of dumboy, or pounded cassava.**

COOKSHOPS

Cookshops are small stalls that can be found all over Liberia's cities. They sell delicious and nutritious food at affordable prices. Fried banana or plantain fritters and rice-based dishes are popular cookshop fare. Many cookshops serve a meal of rice accompanied by a dish that consists of cabbage cooked with pork or fish cooked with sweet potato leaves.

Another important staple is cassava, which can be eaten boiled, fried, or in the form of *dumboy* (DUHM-boy). Dumboy is made by cooking fresh cassava and then pounding it until a thick paste is formed. To eat dumboy, it first has to be portioned into managable pieces. Each piece is then dipped in a spicy stew or sauce before it is eaten. Other Liberian staples include sweet potatoes, yams, and eddoes, which are a type of root vegetable.

Vegetables and Fruits

Vegetables are an important part of the Liberian diet. Collard greens, pumpkins, pumpkin leaves, cassava leaves, red peppers, cabbage, sweet potato leaves, okras, and eggplants are available in Liberian markets and are often prepared as parts of home-cooked meals. Other types of vegetables popular with Liberian cooks are "chicken greens," "palava sauce," and "careless greens." These are local varieties of green, leafy vegetables.

Fruits are also popular with Liberians. Pineapples, bananas, mangoes, citrus fruits, papayas, and coconuts are sold in Liberian markets. Liberians eat these fruits on their own or with rice, meats, stews, and dumboy. Stewed mangoes with cloves and coconut pies are popular Liberian desserts. Liberians also enjoy U.S.-style apple or pumpkin pies.

PALM OIL AND COUNTRY CHOP

Oil palm trees grow in parts of Liberia, and palm oil is extracted from the fruits of these trees. Palm oil is used to make a dish called country chop, which consists of cooking one of various types of meat or fish and green vegetables in palm oil. The red-colored palm oil gives a distinctive taste and color to the food that is cooked in it. Country chop is usually served over rice and garnished with a choice of several foods, usually including hard-boiled eggs, onions, shredded coconut, and sliced fruit.

A CLOSER LOOK AT LIBERIA

For much of the nineteenth century, the American Colonization Society helped thousands of freed African American slaves immigrate from the United States to Liberia. The new immigrants, or Americo-Liberians, formed the Republic of Liberia in 1847 and began to blend with the variety of indigenous cultures in the region. Today, Liberia is struggling to keep peace at home and with its neighbors and to manage its resources, which offer economic opportunities. Liberia's natural resources do not end with valuable commodities. The country is also home to a remarkably rich bird life; the pygmy hippopotamus, a vulnerable

Opposite: **Liberia lacks safe drinking water. In Monrovia, civil-war fighting damaged the central water supply and sewage disposal systems in 1992. Water supplies to some central parts of Monrovia have since been restored, but many Liberians still depend on water that has been hand-pumped from wells.**

species; and untouched ancient forests. Joseph Jenkins Roberts and William Tubman, Liberia's first and seventeenth presidents, respectively, made valuable contributions to the nation and have indelibly marked the country's history. Traditional indigenous Liberian cultures, including the Vai, Bassa, Kpelle, and Dan, are gaining new interest and respect in Liberia and around the world. Liberia's rich storytelling traditions include many colorful folktales, which have since been retold and preserved in modern-day books such as *Head, Body, Legs* and *Mrs. Chicken and the Hungry Crocodile*.

Above: **The Oriental Timber Company opened a factory in Buchanan in 2002. Here, factory workers stack sheets of plywood for export.**

The American Colonization Society

In December 1816, a group of influential Americans decided to form the American Colonization Society (ACS). ACS aimed to send free black people to Africa's western coast to establish colonies. Bushrod Washington, nephew of George Washington, was the society's first president.

Mixed Motives

ACS, somewhat ironically, received support from both racially prejudiced and white Americans who were sympathetic to black Americans suffering because of racism. Henry Clay, an ACS founding participant, believed that African-Americans "never could amalgamate with the free whites of this country" in the face of "unconquerable prejudice resulting from their color." For other ACS supporters, the prospect of sending free African-Americans to Africa had less to do with hopes for life without prejudice for the ex-slaves. Robert Finley, an ACS founder and a minister,

Below: **This is an artist's impression of African Americans waiting to depart for Liberia in the 1880s.**

believed that freed slaves would only fulfill their true potential if they lived in Africa. He also thought that sending Christian African Americans to Africa would help spread Christianity throughout the continent. Many prejudiced Americans approved of sending freed slaves to Africa because they feared social conditions they deemed undesirable, including interracial marriages and having to support poor African Americans.

The African American Reaction

Influential African Americans, including ministers and businesspeople, supported ACS because they believed that African Americans could not live happy lives in the United States due to the discrimination they faced. Some African Americans also saw the emigration scheme as a way of spreading Christianity in Africa. The majority of ordinary African Americans, however, were unimpressed with ACS. Some feared that all African Americans would one day be forced to leave the United States, while others feared that if more and more African Americans chose to go to West Africa, then few would be left to help campaign against slavery in the southern part of the United States.

Above: **The ACS continued to send emigrants to Liberia even after the colony became independent. By the 1870s, the society had sent more than 12,000 African Americans to Liberia. With the abolition of slavery in the United States, the work of the society came to a standstill. The ACS was not officially closed until 1964, when its assets were transferred to the Phelps-Stokes Fund, a society that supports African and African American education.**

Birds of Liberia

Liberia is home to remarkably diverse bird life. Ornithologists, or scientists who study birds, have begun only recently to closely study Liberia's birds, as well as their subspecies, habitats, habits, and lifecycles. In their studies, ornithologists have discovered new species of birds in Liberia that have yet to be identified anywhere else in the world. They have sighted 637 species of birds belonging to sixty-seven families in the country. Thirteen of these species of birds, however, are endangered, and sixteen are only found in three or fewer African countries.

Diverse Habitats, Diverse Bird Life

In Liberia, bird life is particularly rich in several areas, including the small, rocky islands that lie off the eastern section of the coastline; the lagoons, mangrove swamps, rivers, and rice fields in the country's coastal areas; and the savannas, forests, rivers, and mountains of the country's vast, inland interior.

The lagoons and mangrove swamps support the unique, white-faced whistling duck, among numerous others. The country's river habitats are home to many herons and migratory birds such plovers and skimmers. Birds typically seen in the country's river areas include the African skimmer, the white-crowned lapwing, and the white-throated blue swallow. Rivers and rice fields form ideal homes for snipes, sandpipers, and herons during winter, while yellow wagtails and swallows tend to favor coffee and cocoa plantations.

The savanna birds of Liberia's inland areas include the African warbler, the kingfisher, the little bee-eater, and the pin-tailed whydah. Colorful forest birds include hornbills, broad-billed rollers, and the yellow-whiskered greenbul. The hornbill family is a good example of great diversity within one family. Eight subspecies of hornbills have been found in Liberian forests. They range in size, with some more than 3 feet (1 m) long and others no bigger than a thrush. Some experts consider the rare black-and-white casqued hornbill a ninth subspecies.

Commercial logging is the most serious threat to bird life in Liberia. Rapid deforestation is leading to dwindling wilderness areas and, consequently, fewer natural habitats for the birds.

Above and *opposite*: The pepper bird (*Pycnonotus barbatus*) is Liberia's national bird and is known for a loud, shrill call that often wakes people up at dawn. A species of bulbul, the pepper bird has been nicknamed the "alarm clock of West Africa." Legend has it that every night people dream and sleep peacefully in the arms of Father Night, who wants to stay as long as he can. At dawn, however, the pepper bird tells Father Night that Father Day has arrived so that people can go to work as a new day begins. Father Night at first ignores the pepper bird, so it shrieks louder and louder until Father Night can no longer stand the noise and releases the people over to Father Day.

Dan Masks

The Dan are one of Liberia's ethnic groups and a branch of the larger Mande family. Also known as Gio or Yakuba, the Dan typically inhabit northeastern Liberia. Dan communities also exist in neighboring Côte d'Ivoire, or Ivory Coast. The Dan tend to settle in isloated, mountainous areas, where they grow cassava and rice on the slopes. Despite their relatively reclusive lifestyle, the Dan enjoy a good reputation around the world for the beautiful hardwood masks that they carve. The masks are called *gle* (GLAY) in the Dan language. Other Dan arts include other types of carvings, storytelling, and mural paintings.

Gle play an important role in Dan religious ceremonies. They are only worn by dancers when performing religious rites and rituals, and the Dan believe that the wearer of a mask takes on the spirit of the figure the mask represents. Often, the masks represent famous Dan ancestors who once held power in the community. When such masks are worn, the Dan believe that they can recall the power of these ancestors to maintain control and balance in their society.

A SACRED ART

Only specially trained Dan are allowed to carve masks. Dan boys have to spend many years learning the art form under the guidance of their Poro elders. The boys are only allowed to carve masks when they have graduated from the Poro society and become adults. The Dan believe that masks should be carved only when they dream of spirits who have asked them for a physical form.

Below: Two Dan children and a tribal elder pose for a photograph before their ritual dance.

Left: Dan masks are painted with a vegetable extract that resembles lacquer when it dries. The shiny finish helps to highlight the beautiful carved features.

Female and Male Masks

Dan masks can represent either male or female beings, although Dan women can never wear masks. Female masks are most often used in public rituals to judge disputes or to protect children. Carved differently than male masks, female masks have oval foreheads, long, narrow slits for eyes, and small noses and mouths. Some Dan families keep reproductions of female masks at home for protection against disease. Palm oil, rice, and other sacrifices are offered to female masks during certain periods of the year as a sign of devotion.

Male Dan masks usually look more lifelike than female masks and sometimes include a mixture of human and animal features. Male masks represent *du* (DOO), which are spirits of strength. The Dan believe that du appear in their dreams and ask people to perform certain actions. Du have been believed to ask for trees to be planted or masks to be carved so that they can live in them. For the Dan, the du can take part in everyday Dan life, including celebrations and important social events, once they enter their requested forms or objects.

OTHER USES OF DAN MASKS

Dan masks are also made to represent spirits or ancestors who can offer petitions or thanksgiving to the gods on behalf of the people. The masks are believed to act as the people's agents of the gods. Other Dan masks are believed to represent the figure or force of punishment for acts of wrongdoing. A colorful mask decorated with metal pieces, cowrie shells, bells, netting, beads, and a large hat, the *Ga Wree Wree* (GAH woo-REE woo-REE), might be worn by a community chief when he is judging disputes or punishing someone who has committed a crime.

On a lighter note, the *Ma Na Gle* (MAH nah GLAY), also known as the "bird mask," is decorated with colorful cloth, metal pieces, and cowrie shells. The wearer of the "bird mask" dances and sings in honor of the parakeet and the hornbill.

Diamonds: A Controversial Resource

Liberia is rich in many precious metals and minerals, including diamonds. The reputation of Liberian diamonds has been tainted, however, by allegations that the country's diamond trade has been fueling armed conflict in West Africa in recent years.

Liberia produces two types of diamonds: industrial and gem. Industrial diamonds are used to make tools that can cut through rock or other hard materials, as well as those used to smooth and polish rough stone surfaces. Gem diamonds are used to make jewelry. Liberia's diamond resources have been estimated at about 10 million carats. Carats are the universal units of measure for precious stones, and one carat weighs about 200 milligrams.

Funding Civil Wars

Because diamond production increased during the civil war, many people believed that Liberian warlords who had gained control of diamond mines were mining diamonds to finance their sustained military operations in the country.

Below: **During the civil war, rival factions fought bitterly with each other to control the country's various diamond mines. Diamonds in Liberia were discovered in the late 1950s near the lower reaches of the Loffa River, where they were found in both kimberlite and alluvium deposits. The river areas in Nimba, Montserrado, and Grand Bassa counties are also known sources of alluvial diamonds.**

Left: Two teenagers in eastern Sierra Leone, near the border of Liberia, continued to dig for diamonds in 2002 even though the United Nations had banned the sale of all diamonds from the country.

During the civil war, Liberia not only produced more diamonds, but also became a transit point for diamonds from neighboring Sierra Leone, which was also in the throes of a bloody civil war. Warlords are believed to have purchased weapons with diamond proceeds for war efforts in Sierra Leone. Diamonds from both countries, as a result, came to be known as "conflict diamonds."

Sanctions

In 2000, United Nations (UN) authorities had reasons to believe that the sale of "conflict diamonds" was increasing the amount of weapons surfacing in West Africa and, thereby, escalating the unrest in the region. They passed a law banning trade of all diamonds from Sierra Leone. In 2001, the UN Security Council moved to ban all diamonds from Liberia because there was evidence to suggest that Sierra Leonean diamonds were smuggled into Liberia to reach the international market. UN authorities have since stated that they would lift sanctions on Liberia's diamond industry if the government adopts a proper certification process supported by the international community.

THE KIMBERLEY PROCESS

The World Diamond Council was set up in 2000 to eliminate the trading of "conflict diamonds." The council launched the Kimberley Process, which combined the efforts of thirty-eight governments; the chairmen of the United Nations sanctions committees for Angola and Liberia, the European community, and several nongovernmental organizations to prevent "conflict diamonds" from reaching world markets. Effective January 1, 2003, the Kimberley Process Certification Scheme demands a certificate of origin and authenticity for each diamond, as well as a declaration stating that the diamond is from sources not involved in funding military conflict. Liberia did not sign on when the process was introduced.

Indigenous Alphabets

Liberia is home to many ethnic groups, each with their own language and dialects. Although most indigenous languages are only used for speaking, a few exceptions, including the Vai and Bassa languages, have written scripts, or alphabets.

Vai Language and Literacy

Tha Vai script is a syllabary, which means that each symbol represents a syllable rather than a letter or a word. For example, there is one symbol each for the sounds of "pah," "pay," "pee," "paw," and "poh." Characters used in the syllabary include triangles, s-shapes, dots, circles, straight and wavy lines, crosses, and oval and diamond shapes. A page of text in the Vai script is a beautiful piece of calligraphic art that includes many different geometric shapes, symbols, and swirls. In 1962, the University of Liberia standardized the Vai syllabary.

Linguists and anthropologists who have studied the Vai language and script to better understand the Vai people's use of writing discovered that educated Vai use up to three languages in their everyday life: English to write official letters, Arabic to read the Qur'an, and Vai to write personal letters and record

Hwɛ̀ ɓɛ́ ɖɛ séén ké ma nìɛɛ. Wuɖuɔ̀ nì ma. ɔ nì ma ɓó Gèɖèpɔɔ̀ gbo, ké ɔ kè Gèɖèpɔ́ɔ̀ mɔ̀ ma nyɔ dyuáɖò. Dé ɖɛ gbɔ-dè-dè múɛɛ, Wuɖuɔ̀ nì ma ɓó Gèɖèpɔ́ɔ̀ gbo. Ké dyììn ɖé ɔ múɛɛ, Gèɖèpɔ́ɔ̀ nyu ma ɖɛ séén. ɔ se ma mú nììn, Gèɖèpɔ́ɔ̀ se ma ɖɛ ɓè ɓɛ́ ɔ nyu ma kà kɛɛ, dyuáɖò nyuɛ ɓɛ́ɛ̀n. Fɛ̀ɛ̀ nì ma ɖɛ́ Wuɖuɔ̀ mú, ké fɛ̀ɛ̀ nà kɛɛ nyu, ké nyɔɔ̀n-dyù ɓéɖé ma ce. Ceɔ̀ fȁàin ɖɛ́ tíe-kpòɔ̀ mú, ké tíe-kpòɔ̀ seɛ mɔ́ɔ̀ɛ̀n. Gèɖèpɔ́ɔ̀ tò ma gàa ɖò kɔ̀ nyɛ́nɛ́ mɔ̀ ma Jɔ̃́ɔ́ kɛ.

business transactions. Most Vai, however, use the Vai language only in conversation, and only about 28 percent of Vai adult males can read and write at all. About 90,000 people speak the Vai language today.

Reviving the Bassa Script

The Bassa language belongs to the Kwa family of languages and is spoken by about 350,000 Liberians. Written Bassa has an indigenous script that gradually fell out of use in Liberia during the 1800s. In the early 1900s, however, Dr. Flo Darvin Lewis, a researcher, discovered that the Bassa script was still being used by Bassa communities in Brazil and the West Indies. These Bassa descended from Liberian slaves who had been brought to the New World. Dr. Lewis decided to learn Bassa himself and then reintroduce the script in Liberia, where he later set up a school to teach the indigenous script. Dr. Lewis also managed to acquire a printing press, with which he produced reading materials written in the Bassa script. The script is most popular among the older generation of Bassa speakers. Today, the Bassa Vah Association of Liberia tries to preserve the Bassa script.

The N'ko Alphabet

Invented in 1949 by Souleymane Kanté, a Guinean man, the N'ko alphabet is another example of an indigenous African script. Although it was not developed in Liberia, the script was designed to help all Mande speakers write in their language. Today, the Association for the Education and Teaching of the N'ko Alphabet in Monrovia promotes the teaching of the N'ko alphabet in Liberia.

Joseph Jenkins Roberts

Liberians are very proud of their first president, Joseph Jenkins Roberts (1809–1876). Under Roberts, Liberia not only extended its borders, but also gained international recognition.

Born in the United States in Norfolk, Virginia, Joseph Jenkins Roberts worked for his father and trained as a barber. Roberts's father owned boats that transported goods on the James and Appomattox rivers. The family accumulated an unusual amount of money and property for the times. In 1823, Roberts's father died, and the Roberts family decided to move to Liberia. In 1829, with help from the American Colonization Society (ACS), the Roberts family sailed to Liberia aboard the ship *Harriet*.

A New Life in Monrovia

Letters written by Amelia, Roberts's mother, from Liberia indicate that the family was pleased with its new life in Monrovia. Roberts had set up a trading company with a friend and was transporting African goods, such as ivory, camwood, and animal hides, to various ports in the United States. The business was a success partly because Roberts maintained good relations with both the

Below: **This is an artist's impression of President Roberts's home in the 1870s. Today, Roberts is fondly remembered as a distinguished leader and diplomat who established economic and political stability for Liberia during the early decades of the new republic.**

traders and the indigenous peoples with whom he traded. Roberts's diplomatic skills impressed ACS officials, and they appointed him high sheriff of the Liberian colony in 1833. Roberts proved adept at handling problems and disputes between the colonists and the indigenous Africans. By 1839, he was appointed lieutenant governor and, in 1842, he became the colony's first black governor. The biggest honor, however, came in 1848, when Roberts was inaugurated as the first president of Libera.

Presidential Achievements

Roberts served as president from 1847 to 1856 and again from 1872 to 1876. During his first term in office, Liberia's boundaries were extended until they stretched along the Atlantic coast for nearly 600 miles (965 km). Roberts was able to use a combination of diplomacy and force to achieve peace with the inland indigenous groups. He also traveled to Europe to secure formal recognition for newly independent Liberia. By the early 1850s, the first African republic was acknowledged by some of Europe's major powers, including England, France, Portugal, Austria, Sweden, and Denmark. The United States recognized Liberia as an independent nation in 1862.

LIBERIA COLLEGE

Founded in the 1850s, Liberia College was the republic's first institution of higher learning. Joseph Jenkins Roberts served not only as the college's first president, but also as a professor of jurisprudence and international law. Four other Liberian presidents — Garretson Gibson, Arthur Barclay, Charles King, and Edward Barclay — also served at the college, which became the University of Liberia in 1951.

The Kpelle

The largest ethnic group in Liberia, the Kpelle speak a language of the Mande family. Other Mande peoples in Liberia include the Loma, Gbandi, Gio, Vai, and Mano.

Kpelle Settlements

The Kpelle of Liberia live mainly in Bong County and other parts of central Liberia, where the land is generally divided between rain forests and hills in the upland areas and swamps and rivers in lowland areas. The Kpelle live in villages, which can include from 10 to 150 homesteads. Important villages and those along paved roads have the largest populations. Some Kpelle and their families choose to live away from the larger villages, preferring surroundings of open bushland. In Monrovia and other large cities, urban Kpelle communities formed in the 1960s and 1970s, when many migrated to cities in search of jobs. The civil war in the 1990s drove many Kpelle from their villages to Monrovia and the country of Guinea, where they live as refugees today.

MANDE ANCESTRY AND DIVERSITY

A large and diverse group, Mande peoples are descendants of the great Mali Empire, a trading empire that flourished in West Africa along the Mali-Guinea border between the 1200s and the 1500s. Today, Mande peoples live in Burkina Faso, Guinea, Senegal, Gambia, Guinea-Bissau, Sierra Leone, Liberia, Côte d'Ivore, and Ghana.

Below: Kpelle settlements in rural parts of Liberia look much like this one shown here.

Left: These Liberians are standing next to their rice farm. Labor is divided according to gender in traditional Kpelle life. Men are responsible for clearing land, hunting, and gathering palm and kola nuts. Women are in charge of planting and fishing, as well as gathering vegetables, wild fruits, herbs, and roots. Both women and men practice weaving, but they make different items. Women mostly weave fishing nets and baskets, while men make furniture and mats.

Kpelle Economy and Society

The rural Kpelle are mainly farmers. Rice and cassava are cultivated as staple foods. Other crops include yams, potatoes, plaintains, eggplants, peanuts, tomatoes, and peppers. Some Kpelle farmers grow fruits, including pineapples, mangoes, bananas, and oranges. Increasing numbers of Kpelle earn their livings working on rubber farms or in mines.

Traditional Kpelle society is divided into associations. The *kuu* (KOOH), for example, is an informal group of family, friends, and neighbors who assemble to clear forests for growing rice or building houses. The kuu also gather for other work and communal activities. The Sande and Poro, which are cultural associations for women and men, respectively, function as religious, social, political, legal, and educational institutions. Separate groups govern specialized activities, such as making medicines or controlling snakes. The Kpelle do not have a large political organization governing the entire group. Paramount chiefs are the highest local government officials, and they supervise district chiefs, who, in turn, oversee town chiefs.

KPELLE RELIGION

Between 10 and 25 percent of Kpelle are Christian and a small percentage are Muslim. Most Kpelle practice traditional African religions. They believe in a god who created Earth, and in a large variety of spirits, especially those that are believed to live in masks. Religious rituals are carried out by the Sande and Poro.

Liberian Folktales

Storytelling and the Storyteller

Storytelling is very much a part of everyday Liberian life, especially in rural Liberia. In rural areas, storytelling sometimes involves music, drumming, and dancing. In West African cultures, storytellers are highly regarded and are often considered as entertainers, teachers, and guardians of historical and traditional knowledge, all rolled into one. Some West African cultures call their storytellers *griots* (GREE-yohs). Liberia's Dan people call their storytellers *tlo ker mehn* (tee-loh care MAIN).

Characters in Liberian Folktales

Liberian folktales are often about animals and insects, including spiders, rabbits, leopards, lions, and fireflies. *The Great Race*, for example, is about a race between a deer and a turtle. Animal characters featured in Liberian folktales are typically portrayed as having specific human qualities. The rabbit, for example, is usually portrayed as cunning.

Below, left and *right:* **Many of Liberia's traditional folktales have been written down and published for readers around the world to enjoy. Liberian folktales are among some of the most colorful stories from West Africa and often serve as an excellent way to introduce people to Liberian culture and history.**

MORE LIBERIAN FOLKTALES

Liberian folktales feature some delightful characters, including a greedy spider that ate so much it became fat and got stuck in a tree; a man and a woman, each with only one eye, one ear, one leg, and one foot; a clever rooster that outwitted a snake; and a wise chief who had an even wiser wife.

FOLKTALES AS CULTURE, HISTORY, AND RELIGION

Today, researchers and academics consider folktales and stories to be important parts of the cultures and histories of particular groups of people. Such stories show how different cultures view the world around them and what they consider important in their respective societies. Important historical events are also captured in folktales and stories. Many African societies tell stories about where they come from, who they believe created them, and events that influenced them. Religious stories educate people about societies' religious beliefs and help preserve their traditions and cultures.

Liberian folktales are also often about people or how people relate to animals and nature. Many such stories are told to teach people how to behave, with the bad characters usually punished by the end of the story. Human characters in Liberian folktales commonly turn out to be spirits or animals disguised as humans. In the story of Wana, a crocodile disguises itself as a woman. In another story, the hunter who only hunted elephants encountered an elephant that turned into a beautiful woman.

Modern Liberian Folktales

Because folktales and storytelling are at the center of Liberian culture, modern folktales have been invented and told to young Liberians in an effort to help them recover from the effects of the bloody civil war. International organizations, such as Women's Rights International and Women's Health and Development Program, for example, have developed a program using folktales and stories to educate the public about violence against women during the civil war. The program helps female victims of violence to overcome their fears and teaches the public that they have access to help if they are victims of violence.

Logging and the Environment

Liberia is home to some of the last remaining ancient forests in West Africa. Collectively known as the Upper Guinea Forest ecosystem, the ancient forests once covered all of Liberia and areas in Guinea, Sierra Leone, Côte d'Ivoire, Ghana, and Togo. Today, Liberia is the only country that has a significant proportion of the original forest cover intact. Indiscriminate logging, however, is causing Liberia's forests to rapidly dwindle.

Logging Companies

In the past, the slash-and-burn practices of Liberian farmers contributed to deforestation and the destruction of animal habitats and ecosystems. In the last thirty years, however, commercial logging has been a far greater problem, causing a dramatic loss of forests in Liberia. Commercial logging is carried out by both local and international logging companies, which export the timber to countries such as France, Italy, and

GREENPEACE

In 2002, Greenpeace, an international organization that works to protect the environment, staged several protests (*above*) to call attention to the problems of Liberian forests. Activists boarded ships at a Greek port to stop their cargoes of Liberian timber from being unloaded. The protests highlight Greenpeace's demand for a ban on the trading of Liberian timber in order to save the last remaining forests in the Upper Guinea Forest ecosystem in West Africa.

Left: **About 45 percent of the forests in West Africa are found in Liberia. It is believed, however, that Liberia's forests will disappear in between ten and twenty years if logging continues at the present rate.**

China. The Liberian government has granted to these companies logging rights to exploit a total of over 7.4 million acres (3 million hectares). This area amounts to about 62 percent of Liberia's remaining forests. The Oriental Timber Company has been granted the right to harvest over 30 percent of Liberian forests.

Above: **Two employees of the Inland Logging Company stand by their truck in Juazohn, Singe County.**

Timber — Another Controversial Resource

Liberian timber, like the country's diamonds, is a controversial resource, but for a variety of different reasons. Logging is carried out with little to no regard for Liberia's environment. Motivated by short-term profits, the logging companies cut down all trees regardless of their size or the quality of the wood. Once the trees disappear, so does all the animal and plant life once dependent on them. Logging also displaces forest-dwelling, indigenous communities. Despite the huge sacrifices, the regions that have been exploited actually receive little of the income from the timber exports. Taxes collected from the logging companies, instead, go straight into the government's treasury.

Mining

The mining industry has long been one of the main engines of the Liberian economy. Although iron ore production has ceased, the iron ore mining industry fueled the Liberian economy in the 1960s and 1970s. Today, gold is the focus of Liberia's recovering mining industry.

Mining Iron Ore

Operated by the Liberian Mining Company, Liberia's first iron ore mine opened at Bomi Hills in 1951. Over the next two decades, many more companies opened iron ore mines in various parts of Liberia. By the mid-1960s, Liberia's largest iron ore deposits had been discovered, and the country became one of the world's top exporters of iron ore.

In the 1980s, world prices for iron ore fell and remained low, slowly choking Liberia's iron ore mining industry. The greatest blow to the industry, however, was dealt in 1989, when the country's civil war began. Many large mines, including those near the Nimba Range and the Bong Mines, ceased production almost immediately. Efforts to reopen the Nimba

Left: Today, the Yekepa Mine area in Nimba County resembles a ghost town. Its quiet appearance belies the bustling mining activity that took place there in the 1960s and 1970s.

mines in the early 1990s met with limited success; the iron ore deposits there were soon exhausted, and no large-scale iron ore production has since taken place in the country. The war also destroyed much of the civil infrastructure of the larger mining towns, such as Bong Town and Yekepa.

Above: The Yekepa Mine and other major mines in Nimba County were briefly reopened in the early 1990s.

Mining Gold

Gold mining has become much more important in Liberia since the country's iron ore production has diminished. Significant deposits of gold have been found near Tchien, or Zwedru, in Grand Gedeh County; between the Mano and Loffa rivers in western Liberia; along St. John River in Bong County; and in parts of southeastern Liberia. During the civil war, rival factions fought to gain control over the gold mines, and money from gold mining was rumoured to be funding their war efforts. Since the end of the civil war, Liberia's gold production has increased because of investments from large foreign companies, such as Mano River Resources and Amalia Gold, companies based in Canada and South Africa, respectively.

Monrovia

Monrovia is the capital of Liberia and also the country's largest city. Part of Montserrado County, Monrovia is home to the country's main port, which rests on the northwestern coastline of Bushrod Island, facing the Atlantic Ocean. Encircling the city is the Mesurado River, which is one of the tributaries of the St. Paul River.

As Liberia advanced politically and economically, urban centers such as Monrovia, Buchanan, Gbarnga, and Voinjama developed. Founded in 1822, Monrovia was named after U.S. president James Monroe. By 1986, the city had a population of about 450,000, which doubled by 1992, as thousands of refugees poured into the city to escape civil war strife in other parts of the country. In 2000, the population of Monrovia was estimated at more than 1.4 million, and more than one-third of all Liberians lived within an 80-kilometer (50-mile) radius of the city.

Below: **Shops in Monrovia come in a range of shapes and sizes. Elegant boutiques are located close to roadside stalls, while air-conditioned supermarkets compete with noisy, colorful, open-air markets. Many tailors operate roadside stalls that display beautiful, traditional African textiles. Other stalls sell handicrafts, such as jewelry, masks, carvings, and traditional dolls.**

Important Buildings and Monuments

Some of Monrovia's important buildings include the Capitol, the Executive Mansion, the City Hall, and the Temple of Justice. Other important landmarks include the University of Liberia, the John F. Kennedy Memorial Hospital, and the modern Monrovia Consolidated School System complex. Monrovia also is home to the National Museum of Liberia and the National Public Library.

Nightlife and Entertainment

With relative peace in and around Monrovia, residents try to enjoy life as much as possible. Bars, restaurants, discotheques, and hotels are all part of Monrovia's colorful nightlife. Young people gather at these establishments to dance, eat, and enjoy each other's company. Restaurants in Monrovia serve a wide range of food, including African, European, Lebanese, American, Chinese, and traditional Liberian dishes. Gurley Street is the center of Monrovia's nightlife and entertainment.

CULTURAL CENTERS

One of the most famous cultural centers in Liberia is the National Cultural Center in Kendeja, near Monrovia. The National Cultural Troupe, which is made up of dancers from Liberia's various ethnic groups, is based at the Center. Visitors to the Center can watch traditional dances or demonstrations of crafts such as pottery-making and woodcarving. The Center also displays the architectural styles of Liberia's diverse ethnic groups. Other cultural centers near Monrovia are the Malima and Besao villages, where visitors can experience Liberia's traditional foods and dances.

The River Horse

Hippopotamuses are often called "river horses" because the word "hippopotamus" comes from the Greek words *"hippos"* and *"potamios,"* which mean "horse" and "river," respectively. Hippopotamuses, or hippos, are native only to Africa, where two main species exist. Also known as the great river hippo, the Nile hippo (*Hippopotamus amphibius*) mostly inhabits the rivers and lakes of sub-Saharan Africa. The second main species of hippo is called the pygmy hippo (*Hexaprotodon liberiensis*), and it is found in small numbers throughout West Africa, including in Liberia.

The pygmy hippo is noticeably different from its larger relative, the Nile hippo. Apart from being smaller in size, the pygmy hippo's eyes are on the sides of its head, unlike the Nile hippo's eyes, which are on top of its head. In addition, the pygmy hippo's hooves are less webbed than the hooves of the Nile hippo. An average pygmy hippo weighs between 355 and 600 pounds (161 and 272 kilograms), while an average Nile hippo weighs between 2,425 and 5,730 pounds (1,100 and 2,597 kg).

SWEATING BLOOD?

A pygmy hippo has an extremely tough and thick hide, but the upper layer of its hide, or epidermis, is thin. This thin layer absorbs water readily and keeps the animal cool when it is out of the water. The animal also secretes a pinkish fluid from glands beneath its skin to regulate its body temperature. This thick substance also protects the hippo from the harmful ultraviolet rays of the sun. The pink color of the secretions sometimes resembles blood, which is why the pygmy hippo may appear to be sweating blood!

Left: The average length of a pygmy hippo is between 5 and 5.6 feet (1.5 to 1.7 m), and the average height from its shoulder to the ground is between 30 and 39 inches (76 and 99 centimeters). Pygmy hippos are typically found in the tropical regions of West Africa. Small groups of pygmy hippos exist in Guinea, Côte d'Ivoire, Sierra Leone, and possibly Guinea-Bissau. It is only in Liberia, however, that the animal appears in any significant numbers.

Habitats and Habits

Pygmy hippos tend to inhabit lowland forest areas that have many rivers and swamps. While Nile hippos usually submerge themselves in water, pygmy hippos venture into the water only occasionally. Pygmy hippos must, however, stay close to water or suffer dehydration. Solitary and nocturnal creatures, pygmy hippos seek shelter in forested areas during the day. At night, they emerge to search for food, which for them includes fruits, roots, grasses, shoots, and leaves.

Threats and Conservation

The greatest threat facing pygmy hippos in Liberia today is the loss of their lowland forest habitats. As forests are cleared for farming and human settlement, the animals are driven away and often die when they cannot find clean water. Pygmy hippos are also hunted to some extent. The Liberian government has taken some steps to protect the habitats of pygmy hippos. In 1988, pygmy hippos and their habitats became protected by law under the Wildlife and National Park Act. In practice, however, these laws are only effective within Sapo National Park.

Above, left and *right:* **Alexander Peal is a leading Liberian conservationist. Founded by Peal, the Society for the Conservation of Nature of Liberia recently teamed up with the Liberian government and international environmental agencies to start a community-based conservation program at Sapo National Park. The program aims to train Liberians in conservation work, and it is hoped that such programs will help save vulnerable Liberian species, including the pygmy hippo, from extinction.**

Rubber

The rubber industry was an integral part of the Liberian economy during the second half of the twentieth century. In the 1980s, at the peak of rubber production, rubber provided as much as U.S. $110 million in export earnings and employed up to 50,000 Liberians. The Firestone Tire and Rubber Company alone employed some 7,000 Liberians, the largest private-sector workforce in Liberia. Rubber production, however, plummeted in the 1990s following the outbreak of the civil war. Today, the Liberian rubber industry is making a slow but steady recovery.

How the Liberian Rubber Industry Began

U.S.-owned Firestone Tire and Rubber Company was behind the first large-scale rubber plantation in Liberia. Based in Akron, Ohio, the company negotiated for three years with the Liberian and U.S. governments to obtain a ninety-nine-year lease on one

Below: **Important rubber companies in Liberia today include the Liberian Agricultural Company, the Salala Rubber Corporation, the Cavalla Rubber Corporation, Kumpulan Guthrie, and Firestone, which has since been acquired by Japanese-owned tire company Bridgestone to form Bridgestone/Firestone.**

million acres (404,694 ha) of land for cultivating rubber. In 1926, the Firestone plantation opened at Harbel and remains to this day the world's largest rubber plantation.

The arrival of the Firestone Tire and Rubber Company in Liberia attracted other foreign rubber firms, which also obtained large plots of land from the Liberian government on which to grow rubber. Soon, Liberians themselves set up rubber plantations, but their operations were usually much smaller than those run by foreign-owned firms. Rubber production was more or less equally divided between local and overseas producers.

The Civil War

The Liberian civil war forced the Firestone plantation to close in 1990. Although production resumed in 1992, operations were brought to another halt when ECOMOG, the military force of ECOWAS, captured Harbel and Buchanan from NPFL, one of the military factions involved in the civil war. The Firestone plantation next reopened in mid-1997. Many other rubber companies also closed during the civil war. Rubber plantations suffered much damage, with many trees cut down for firewood or overtapped by illegal rubber tappers.

Above: **The Bridgestone/Firestone rubber processing plant fell into disuse and some disrepair during the civil war. Since the end of the war, the country's rubber production has been slowly climbing back to prewar levels. In 1999, Liberia's rubber exports earned about U.S. $32 million and, in 2001, about U.S. $70 million.**

Vai Arts

The Vai people belong to the Mande linguistic family, and most live in the area straddling northwestern Liberia and southern Sierra Leone. In Liberia, many Vai settlements are located between the Loffa and Mano rivers in southern Grand Cape Mount County.

Vai Musical Culture

Music is the heart of Vai culture. For the Vai, music is a must at celebrations of birth, initiations into adulthood, marriages, and funerals. In fact, so inseparable is music from Vai culture that specific tunes are allocated to different occupations or tasks. Hunters, midwives, farmers, and storytellers, for instance, each have their own special music for work and leisure. Music also brings Vai people together at the end of the day, when they gather to reflect on the day's events with singing and dancing. The Sande and Poro play active roles keeping Vai musical traditions alive. In teaching Vai girls and boys what is expected of them as adult members of the Vai society, the Sande and Poro also train young singers, dancers, and musicians.

The Vai dance tradition includes several dances and games for children. These dances and games help introduce Vai youngsters to Vai music, culture, social rules, and etiquette. Children spend a lot of time entertaining themselves with these dances and games, which also teach them how to socialize with each other. Games include hide-and-seek. *Den mese tombo* (DANE MAY-say TOHM-boh) is a popular circular dance for young Vai girls.

Left: These young Liberians are performing a traditional dance. Vai girls and boys often entertain themselves with such dances.

The Hunter's Dance

Vai dances often enact scenes from daily life. One such dance is *buke moe-nu tombo* (BYU-kay MOH-ay TOHM-boh), or the Hunter's Dance. Almost like a musical drama, the dance tells the story of a hunting experience from the start of the hunt to the feasting at the end. Each dancer takes on a particular role, whether it is the master hunter, an ordinary hunter, or the chief.

Masquerades

Only the most skillful Vai dancers perform in *tombokefen tombo* (TOHM-boh-KAY-fayn TOHM-boh), or the masquerade dance. Masquerade dancers have to train for many years before they are allowed to perform in public. Masks are an important part of masquerade dances. Made from wood, the masks are usually black in color and resemble human faces that are believed to represent ancestral spirits. Both men and women perform masquerade dances but rarely together. Masquerades tend to be performed by an entirely male or female cast. Masquerades are energetic and fast-paced, and dancers typically take quick short steps on the balls of their feet and move their arms in rapid motions. They also leap and hop around the dance area.

VAI DANCE COSTUMES

Vai dance costumes are colorful creations. In addition to masks, masquerade dancers also decorate their bodies with streams of colorful yarn and coats of raffia string. Performers of other dances often wear headpieces made of wicker wrapped in colorful yarn and raffia. Some dancers also use cane sticks as props, while others strap rattles to their legs.

William Tubman

William Vacanarat Shadrach Tubman (1895–1971) was the seventeenth president of the Republic of Liberia. He served as president for twenty-seven years, from 1944 to 1971. Tubman remains the longest-serving president in the history of Liberia.

A Dedicated Civil Servant

During his long career as a civil servant in the 1920s and the 1930s, Tubman was elected to a local legislative body and served in a variety of roles, including trial judge, public prosecutor, and arbitration referee. Tubman was elected to the Liberian Senate when he was thirty-five years old. As senator, he tried to increase the political rights of indigenous Liberians. In 1937, Tubman became an associate judge in Liberia's Supreme Court and served in that position until 1943. In the following year, Tubman ran for president and won.

THE EARLY YEARS

Tubman was born in Harper in southeastern Liberia. His family was descended from freed African American slaves who had immigrated to Liberia earlier in the century, and they were poor. His father, a stonemason, was a strict disciplinarian who made his children attend daily family prayer services, church services, and the local school.

Tubman became a Methodist lay pastor when he was nineteen years old. While he was a pastor, he also worked as a junior customs collector and gained respect for his honesty and intelligence. Tubman's interest in public service increased, and he studied law during his free time. He passed the exams required to become a lawyer when he was twenty-three years old.

Left: Education was a priority for William Tubman's administration. In 1951, Liberia College became the University of Liberia, and training institutions for primary and secondary school teachers were set up throughout the country. Agricultural stations also were set up around Liberia to teach farmers new and better ways of growing crops and raising livestock.

Contributions to Liberia

As president, Tubman introduced many reforms that had great social, economic, and political impact on Liberia. Under his administration, Liberia granted voting and property rights to all women above the age of twenty-one. Tubman also granted voting rights to indigenous Liberians, who made up a majority of the population, and implemented a national public school system.

Tubman developed Liberia's economy by encouraging the iron ore mining and rubber industries. The industries brought much needed income, with which the government was able to build roads, highways, and other important infrastructure, including Monrovia's hydroelectric plant and water treatment and sewage systems. Tubman's open economic policies attracted foreign investment and helped modernize Liberia. The Liberian Bank of Industrial Development and Investment was established by Tubman's administration to encourage private investment.

Tubman is regarded as one of Liberia's most effective presidents. He maintained firm control on the country and reformed its social, economic, and political life.

Above: Tubman governed Liberia as president until 1971. Although there was some domestic unrest during his time as president, Tubman's administration is seen as relatively peaceful and progressive.

RELATIONS WITH NORTH AMERICA

The Republic of Liberia was founded by African Americans, and the country has since maintained close links to the United States. Liberia's relations with the United States remained close in the twentieth century. The United States has sent much humanitarian and economic aid to Liberia, and there are significant Liberian communities in the United States. The close ties between the two nations also are shown by the popularity of American culture, dress, mannerisms, and figures of speech used in Liberia. Many of Liberia's national symbols, such as its flag, currency, and pledge of allegiance, were inspired by U.S.

Opposite: **Many Liberians displaced by the civil war live in makeshift homes. Several nations, including the United States, Canada, and Japan, have provided humanitarian aid, ranging from food programs to medical services, to help Liberians recover from the effects of the war.**

models. Many places in Liberia are named after U.S. figures, including Monrovia, named after fifth U.S. president James Monroe and the port of Buchanan, named after Thomas Buchanan, Monrovia's first U.S. governor. Some Liberians feel that the United States should do more to help Liberia recover from the effects of civil war.

Canada and Liberia have had very little contact with each other in recent years. Despite some trading activity, no Canadian investments have been made in Liberia as of late 2002. Canada has provided some humanitarian assistance to Liberia.

Above: **Accompanied by a group of adults, an African American child performs a West African dance during Kwaanza celebrations held in Philadelphia in 2002.**

The Early Years

African Americans, both freeborn and freed slaves, helped established the first settlement of the American Colonization Society (ACS) in what became Liberia. Although it suffered several setbacks, the settlement had a school, a library, and commercial and agricultural businesses within a few years and was attracting more immigrants from the United States. The early settlers built their colony to resemble the parts of the United States from which they had come. Houses were made from stone and wood and had verandas, a style similar to buildings in the southern United States. The colonists used U.S. currency, and they dressed and spoke like Americans, as well.

A Bustling Colony

The early settlers maintained close contact with the United States, both through trading and through writing letters. Joseph Jenkins Roberts, who became Liberia's first president, left Virginia for Liberia in the late 1820s. He set up a trading company that brought U.S. goods into Monrovia and exported African goods to U.S. cities such as New York and Philadelphia. Other traders who made their mark included the McGill brothers from Baltimore. The brothers set up stores and warehouses in Monrovia and contributed to the growing prosperity of the colony. By 1847, the new Republic of Liberia was already a bustling trading center.

Left: The influence of American architecture is evident in this nineteenth-century church located in the city of Greenville in Singe County.

Important Personalities

Most, if not all, of the individuals who played important political or economic roles in Liberia's independence movement were from the United States. Many prominent Liberians, including Liberia's first president, traveled back and forth across the Atlantic for commercial or diplomatic reasons. An educator and statesman, Edward Wilmot Blyden, who was born in the U.S. Virgin Islands and immigrated to Liberia in 1851, also traveled frequently to the United States. Blyden made about eight trips to the United States, where he gave speeches at meetings organized by colonization societies and African American groups. He also gave sermons at church meetings. Blyden believed that African Americans had an important role to play in the economic, social, and political development of Africa, and he encouraged African Americans to move to Liberia.

VIRGINIAN PRESIDENTS

Eight presidents of the United States were born in Virginia. Virginia also has produced three Liberian presidents. The first president of Liberia, Joseph Jenkins Roberts, was born in Petersburg, Virginia, in 1809. James Spriggs Payne was born in Richmond, Virginia, and served as president of Liberia from 1868 to 1870 and from 1876 to 1878. The third Liberian president to emerge from Virginia was Anthony William Gardiner, who served as president between 1878 and 1883.

Close Economic and Political Ties

Historically, relations between the Liberian colony and the United States have been close. For twenty-five years, money to run the colony was provided by the ACS, which raised funds in the United States. Letters written by the early colonists to their friends and associates in America also contained requests for food, clothing, and other supplies. The ACS supported the Liberian colony until its independence in 1847, when a constitution modeled on the U.S. constitution was drawn up for the new republic.

During the latter half of the 1800s, Liberia continued to be governed by politicians who had strong links to the United States. Some Liberian presidents, including James Spriggs Payne, Edward Roye, and Anthony William Gardiner, were born in the United States. The U.S. government, however, was slow to

Left: **In May 1943, Brigadier General Ben Davis (*far left*), the highest ranking African American in the U.S. army at the time, Liberian president Edwin Barclay (*second from left*), U.S. representative Sol Bloom (*center*), and future Liberian president William V. S. Tubman (*second from right*) stood outside the Capitol in Washington, D.C. The Liberians were in the United States for an official visit. In 1978, President Jimmy Carter became the first U.S. president to officially visit Liberia.**

Left: **In May 1943, Liberian president Edwin Barclay (*second from left*) and future Liberian president William V. S. Tubman (*second from right*) met with U.S. president Franklin Roosevelt (*center*), first lady Eleanor Roosevelt (*far left*), and U.S. secretary of state Cordell Hull (*far right*) at the White House while on an official visit to the United States.**

recognize the new republic, with formal relations established only in 1862, when the two countries signed a treaty of commerce and navigation.

In the early 1900s, Liberia's finances were reorganized by foreign bankers at the recommendation of U.S. president Theodore Roosevelt. A loan of U.S. $1.7 million was raised for Liberia, and a group of American and European financiers became responsible for administering Liberia's customs income. Liberia's financial situation did not improve, however, and its government was again forced to borrow money. This time, a private U.S. company, the Firestone Tire and Rubber Company, loaned money in return for 1 million acres (404,694 ha) of land on which to plant rubber trees. The company paid the Liberian government a nominal U.S. $0.08 for every acre (0.405 ha) of land. Liberia's internal and customs revenue was then put under the charge of a U.S. financial advisor.

During World War II, Liberia replaced Southeast Asia as the main source of rubber for the Allied forces, and in 1942, the two nations signed a defense treaty, under which the United States agreed to build for Liberia roads leading into the country's inland regions, an international airport, and a deepwater harbor. During the presidency of William Tubman, which lasted from 1944 to 1971, U.S. firms began operations in Liberia's mining industry.

The 1980s and 1990s

The United States donated significant amounts of economic aid to Liberia in the 1980s. The Reagan administration, in particular, donated U.S. $400 million to modernize the Liberian army and to pay for elections in 1985. Liberia received the largest amount of aid given to any African country during that period.

Liberia's civil war erupted in the early 1990s. During that time, many Liberians felt that the U.S. government should have sent troops into Liberia to reestablish peace. The U.S. government did not and, instead, evacuated U.S. citizens and other foreign nationals in Monrovia. Nevertheless, there was still considerable U.S. involvement in helping to establish peace. The Carter Center, a nongovernmental organization founded by former U.S. president Jimmy Carter, was asked by the warring factions in Liberia to help in the peace process.

The Carter Center

The Carter Center opened an office in Monrovia in 1992 and began helping other nongovernmental organizations coordinate their efforts. The Carter Center also started human rights projects and helped prepare the country for the presidential elections in 1997. Led by Jimmy Carter, former Benin president Nicephore

Left: **In August 1982, U.S. president Ronald Reagan (*left*) and chairman of Liberia Samuel Doe (*right*) stood outside the White House looking into the Rose Garden.**

Left: In 1990, not long after the outbreak of the civil war, U.S. soldiers were stationed on the roof of the U.S. embassy in Monrovia as part of increased security measures.

Soglo, and former U.S. senator Paul Simon, the Carter Center monitoring team observed some of Liberia's polling stations and concluded that the elections were free, fair, and legitimate. The Carter Center continued to support programs in Liberia until 2000. It helped train Liberian journalists, provided financial and technical assistance to human rights programs, and established Free Press, Inc., an independent and nonprofit organization owned and jointly run by Liberia's main media companies. Free Press, Inc. manages the printing machinery and processes relating to the actual production of newspapers and other publications.

Into the Twenty-First Century

Relations between Liberia and the United States at the beginning of the twenty-first century are promising. The United States remains the largest donor of aid to Liberia. This aid does not go directly to the Liberian government but to international aid and relief organizations working in Liberia. Some unhappiness remains, however, over the sustained travel bans imposed by the United States on senior Liberian government officials, as well as over the weapons and diamond embargoes that the U.N. Security Council has placed on Liberia. Liberians would also like to see the United States take more of an active role in helping to end the current unrest in their country.

Canada-Liberia Relations

Canada and Liberia have limited formal diplomatic relations, but trade between the two countries is relatively significant. In 2000, Canada exported CAN $1.2 million dollars worth of used clothing, machinery, and vegetables to Liberia and imported CAN $2.8 million dollars worth of natural rubber from the country. As of late 2002, no Canadian business has invested in Liberia. In 1997, Canada pledged U.S. $14 million to help Liberia recover from the civil war. In 2002, the Canadian International Development Agency (CIDA) donated money to a medical organization to assist Liberian refugees in Lofa County.

The Peace Corps in Liberia

Since 1961, the U.S. Peace Corps has been sending volunteers to various developing countries, including Liberia, to help implement a range of programs, including educational, healthcare, and agricultural programs. Between 1961 and 1990, approximately 4,000 volunteers served in Liberia as teachers, financial advisers, healthcare providers, and technicians. The volunteers worked in Monrovia, as well as rural areas such as Voinjama, Sanniquellie, and Tapeta.

AN AMERICAN IN LIBERIA

Hyla S. Watters was an American doctor who worked in Liberia from 1950 to 1961. She was based at Ganta (present-day Gahnpa) in Nimba County, although she traveled widely within Liberia. She learned the languages and customs of the Mano people and was widely respected as a doctor and surgeon. Her published memoirs are a good description of life in northern Liberia in the 1950s.

THE LIBERIAN STUDIES ASSOCIATION

The Liberian Studies Association (LSA) is a U.S. academic organization founded to encourage university-level research on topics related to Liberia. Based at Fayetteville University in North Carolina, the LSA publishes the *Liberian Studies Journal*, which is the second-oldest journal of African studies in the United States. The LSA also supports educational exchanges between the United States and Liberia.

Left: In June 2001, a foreign aid worker was overwhelmed by the sheer number of Liberian refugees in the town of Kailahun in Sierra Leone.

Left: **In April 1998, Italian opera singer Luciano Pavarotti (*center*), U.S. pop singer Stevie Wonder (*left*), and U.S. filmmaker Spike Lee (*right*) posed for a photograph during a press conference promoting Pavarotti's charity concert dedicated to raising money for the children of postwar Liberia. The concert was held in Italy on June 9, 1998.**

Friends of Liberia

A nonprofit nongovernmental organization, Friends of Liberia is based in Washington, D.C. It is dedicated to rebuilding postwar Liberia. Founded by former volunteers of the U.S. Peace Corps who had served in Liberia and returned to the United States, the group has since donated over U.S. $100,000 worth of medical, school, and agricultural supplies to Liberians affected by the war.

Friends of Liberia promotes education in Liberia through the Liberian Education Assistance Program. Every year, experienced U.S. teachers conduct training sessions for Liberian schoolteachers and principals. In 2000, about forty Liberians from Bong, Nimba, and Grand Bassa counties learned to teach schoolchildren mathematics, science, music, languages, and art. Friends of Liberia also supports Sugar Hill Community School in Gbarnga. The school caters to students at primary and secondary levels and has vocational classes in carpentry and sewing for older students. Friends of Liberia is also behind Communities Nurturing Children, a program aimed at improving the standard of living for impoverished Liberian children. The program has, so far, led to the renovation of one clinic and two schools. In addition, Friends of Liberia coordinates women's programs, one of which involved publishing literature on the efforts of Liberian women in promoting peace in their country.

Liberian Communities in the United States

Many Liberians have immigrated to the United States, especially since the civil war began in 1989. While some immigrants have become U.S. citizens, others have chosen to keep their Liberian nationality. Some African Americans have since been born to Liberian parents who emigrated from Liberia to the United States.

Liberians in the United States and Americans of Liberian heritage are a diverse group of people. They work in all fields, including business, education, media, and the arts. The Liberian community in the United States is also ethnically diverse, with many tracing their roots back to different parts of Liberia. Most Liberians who move to the United States settle in the eastern part of the country.

Formed in 1974, the Union of Liberian Associations in the Americas (ULAA) is the umbrella, or unifying, organization for Liberian associations established in about a dozen U.S. states, including Massachusetts, Rhode Island, Ohio, Georgia, and Maryland. Some of the aims of ULAA include promoting peace and reconciliation in Liberia and using the resources of the Liberian community in the United States to help rebuild Liberia.

Below: **In May 1998, United Nations High Commissioner for Refugees Sadako Ogata (*right*) met with some students of Templeton Elementary School in Riverdale, Maryland. The school had a large number of refugee students from all over the world, including Bosnia, Somalia, Iran, Iraq, Liberia, Vietnam, Cuba, Haiti, Sudan, and Ethiopia.**

Protecting Children's Rights

Born in Liberia, Kimmie Weeks is an internationally acclaimed children's rights activist. Although he is based in the United States today, Weeks began his career in human rights in Liberia in 1991. In 1994, Weeks cofounded Voice of the Future, a Liberian nongovernmental organization that works with the United Nations Children's Fund (UNICEF) to provide informal education and health care to children in Liberia. Weeks also founded two other Liberian organizations devoted to children — the Children's Disarmament Campaign and the Children's Bureau of Information. The former calls for the disarmament and rehabilitation of children who fought in the Liberian civil war, while the latter broadcasts radio programs aimed at children, with some of the programs produced by children themselves. In 1999, Kimmie Weeks moved to the United States, where he has continued advocating for children's rights through organizations such as Young Environmental Ambassadors, Youth Action International, and United Nations Manifesto for Peace.

A LIBERIAN IN AMERICA

Samuel Morris was born Prince Kaboo in the 1870s in Liberia. He was captured by an enemy tribe but managed to escape. He found his way to Monrovia, where he became a Christian, and later went to the United States to study to become a missionary. A student at Taylor University in Indiana between 1892 and 1893, he was said to have inspired many people around him. His life was cut short in 1893, when he died of an illness, but the story of his faith helped raise money and support for the university. Today, Taylor University honors the memory of Samuel Morris with a dormitory named after him, as well as sculptures around the campus.

A   B   C   D

	National Boundary
	Provincial Boundary
■	Capital
●	City
○	Town
▲	Mountain
～	River

GUINEA

1

N

Voinjama

Kailahun

Mount Wuteve
(4,528 feet/1,380 m) ▲

Wologizi Range

SIERRA
LEONE

Morro

Mano
Hills

2

LOFA

Yekepa○

Saniquellie

Nimba Range

Mano

Loffa

GPARPOLU

Belefuanai

Gahnpa (Ganta)

GRAND
CAPE
MOUNT

St. Paul

BONG

NIMBA

Bomi Hills

Bong Range

Gbarnga

Cape Mount

BOMI

Robertsport ● Lake Piso

Mesurado

Bong Town ○

St. John

MARGIBI

MONTSERRADO

Kakata

Tapeta

Cess (Cestos)

Cavalla

Bushrod Island →■
MONROVIA

Harbel ○

GRAND
BASSA

3

Tchien (Zwedru) ●

GRAND GEDEH

Buchanan ●

RIVER CESS

ATLANTIC

SINGE

MYERGEE

4

Juazohn ○

OCEAN

Greenville ●

GRAND
KRU

MARY-
LAND

Cape Palmas

Harper ●

5

CÔTE
D'IVOIRE

LIBERIA

Above: Liberians in a remote inland region of the country utilize the limited water resources they have.

Atlantic Ocean A2–D5

Belefuanai C2
Bomi County A2–B3
Bomi Hills A3–B3
Bong County B2–C3
Bong Range B3
Bong Town B3
Buchanan B4
Bushrod Island A3

Cape Mount A3
Cape Palmas D5
Cavalla River D2–D5
Cess (Cestos) River
    B4–D2
Côte d'Ivoire D1–D5

Gahnpa (Ganta) C2
Gbarnga C3
Gparpolu County A2–B2
Grand Bassa County
    B3–C4
Grand Cape Mount
    County A3–B2
Grand Gedeh County
    C3–D4

Grand Kru County
    C4–D5
Greenville C4
Guinea A1–D2

Harbel B3
Harper D5

Juazohn C4

Kailahun B1
Kakata B3

Lake Piso A3
Lofa County B1–C2
Loffa River A3–C1

Mano Hills B2
Mano River A2–B1
Margibi County B3
Maryland County D4–D5
Mesurado River A3–B3
Monrovia A3
Montserrado County
    A3–B3
Morro River A3–B2
Mount Wuteve B2

Myergee (River Gee)
    County C4–D4

Nimba County
    C2–C4
Nimba Range C2

River Cess County
    B4–C3
Robertsport A3

Sanniquellie C2
Sierra Leone A1–B2

Singe (Sinoe)
    County C4
St. John River B4–C2
St. Paul River B3–C1

Tapeta C3
Tchien (Zwedru) D3

Voinjama B1

Wologizi Range B2–C1

Yekepa C2

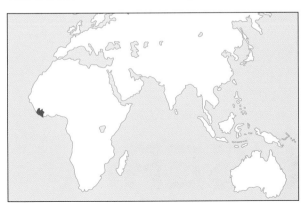

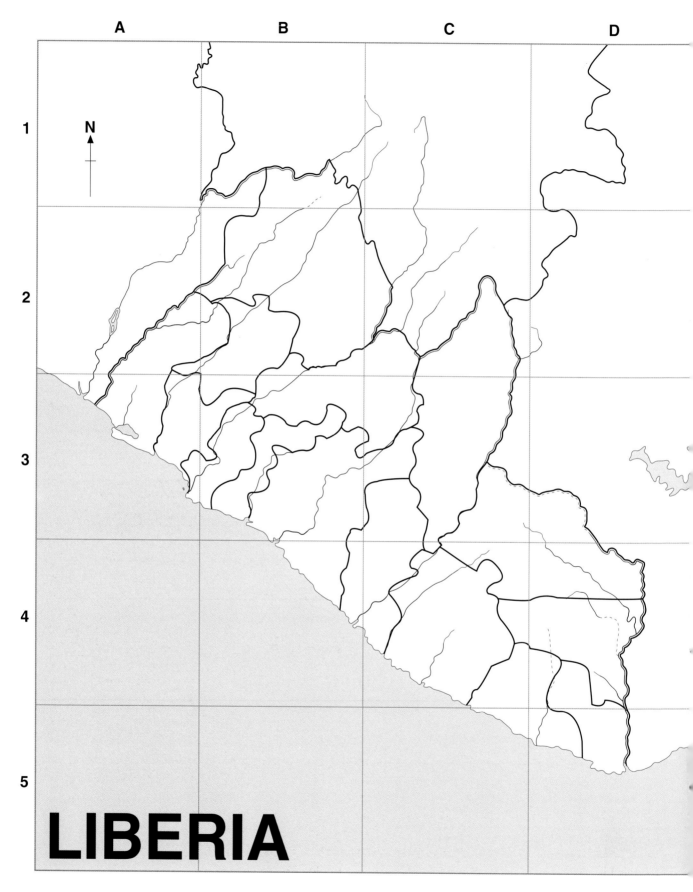

LIBERIA

How Is Your Geography?

Learning to identify the main geographical areas and points of a country can be challenging. Although it may seem difficult at first to memorize the locations and spellings of major cities or the names of mountain ranges, rivers, deserts, lakes, and other prominent physical features, the end result of this effort can be very rewarding. Places you previously did not know existed will suddenly come to life when referred to in world news, whether in newspapers, television reports, other books and reference sources, or on the Internet. This knowledge will make you feel a bit closer to the rest of the world, with its fascinating variety of cultures and physical geography.

Used in a classroom setting, the instructor can make duplicates of this map using a copy machine. (PLEASE DO NOT WRITE IN THIS BOOK!) Students can then fill in any requested information on their individual map copies. Used one-on-one, the student can also make copies of the map on a copy machine and use them as a study tool. The student can practice identifying place names and geographical features on his or her own.

Above: **Liberians displaced by the civil war pose for a photograph outside their home.**

Liberia at a Glance

Official Name   Republic of Liberia

Capital   Monrovia

Official Language   English

Population   3,288,198 (July 2002 estimate)

Total Area   43,000 square miles (111,370 sq km)

Counties   Bomi, Bong, Gparpolu (Gparbolu), Grand Bassa, Grand Cape Mount, Grand Gedeh, Grand Kru, Lofa, Margibi, Maryland, Montserrado, Nimba, River Cess, Myergee (River Gee), Singe (Sinoe)

Highest Point   Mount Wuteve (Wutivi) 4,528 feet (1,380 m)

Border Countries   Côte d'Ivoire, Guinea, Sierra Leone

Major Mountains   Bong Range, Nimba Range, Wologizi Range

Major Rivers   Cavalla, Cess (Cestos), Loffa, Mano, Morro, St. John, St. Paul

Major Lake   Lake Piso

Major Cities   Buchanan, Gbarnga, Greenville, Harbel, Harper, Monrovia, Saniquellie, Tchien (Zwedru), Voinjama

Ethnic Groups   indigenous Africans, Americo-Liberians, Congo People

Main Religions   indigenous beliefs, Christianity, Islam

Main Exports   rubber, timber, diamonds, cocoa, coffee

Main Imports   fuels, chemicals, machinery, transportation equipment, manufactured goods, rice and other foods

Major Trade Partners   Belgium, France, Germany, Italy, Japan, Singapore, South Korea, United States

Currency   Liberian dollar (1 LRD = U.S. $1 in Feb 2003)

Opposite: **A group of Liberians crosses a makeshift bridge to reach their village.**

Glossary

Liberian Vocabulary

balafon (BAH-luh-fawn): a traditional musical instrument that resembles a xylophone.

buke moe-nu tombo (BYU-kay MOH-ay TOHM-boh): a dance of the Vai people; also known as the Hunter's Dance.

damma (DUHM-mah): another name for the *tardegai*.

den mese tombo (DANE MAY-say TOHM-boh): a popular dance among young Vai girls, who must gather in a circle to perform it.

djembe (JEM-bay): a traditional hand drum commonly seen in West Africa and made out of a hollowed tree trunk with animal skin stretched over the top.

djun djun (JOON joon): another name for *dun dun*.

du (DOO): spirits of strength believed in by the Dan culture.

dumboy (DUHM-boy): a staple food made of fresh cassava that is cooked and pounded into a thick paste.

dun dun (DOON doon): bass drums played with sticks that are made of hollowed tree trunks with pieces of hide attached to either end.

Ga Wree Wree (GAH woo-REE woo-REE): the mask a person in authority wears when judging disputes.

gle (GLAY): masks of the Dan people.

griots (GREE-yoh): West African word for storytellers.

jollof (JAW-lof): a dish made from rice, tomatoes, and chicken that can be found in various parts of West Africa. In Liberia, pig's feet, ham, and bacon are sometimes also added.

kboo (POOH): another name for *mancala*.

kono (KOH-noh): a wooden drum with a two-inch lengthwise slit that is played with two sticks.

kora (CORE-rah): a traditional musical instrument popular in West Africa, including Liberia, that features twenty-one strings attached to a calabash, or gourd, base.

kuu (KOOH): an informal group of family members, friends, and neighbors in the Kpelle culture who assemble to clear forests, plant rice, or build houses.

Ma Na Gle (MAH nah GLAY): the mask a person wears to sing and dance in honor of the parakeet and the hornbill; also known as the "bird mask."

mancala (mahn-KAH-lah): a traditional board game played by Liberians.

Poro (POH-roh): a social institution for indigenous men in rural areas that teaches customary law, traditional religion, and proper conduct.

pusava (poo-SAH-vah): imported rice.

Sande (SAHN-day): a social institution for indigenous women in rural areas that teaches customary law, traditional religion, and proper conduct.

sankpah (SUNG-pah): another name for *djembe*.

Tabaski (TAH-BAH-skee): a Muslim festival also known as Eid al-Adha.

tardegai (TAR-duh-GUY): a small, hourglass-shaped drum with ropes attached to its sides.

tlo ker mehn (tee-loh care MAIN): the Dan word for storytellers.

tombokefen tombo (TOHM-boh-KAY-fayn TOHM-boh): a dance of the Vai people, also known as the masquerade dance.

vah (VAH): the Bassa word for their language.

zaza (ZAH-zah): a traditional musical instrument, consisting of a shaker made from dried gourd and decorated with a beautiful net of beads.

English Vocabulary

albeit: although.

allayed: put to rest feelings of fear or anxiety; calmed.

alluvium: clay, silt, sand, gravel, or similar materials deposited by moving water.

atrocities: shockingly wicked, cruel, or brutal acts.

biodiversity: the variety of plant and animal species in an environment.

bureau: a division or branch of a larger government department.

cassava: a type of root vegetable, also known as tapioca.

clan: a group of people united by some common interest.

conservation: the controlled utilization or official supervision of natural resources in order to preserve them, protect them, or prevent their depletion.

coup: an unexpected political takeover.

customs: taxes imposed by law on imported or exported goods.

emblem: an object or design that identifies something; symbol.

favoritism: the choosing of one person or group over others with equal claims.

fraught: filled.

hydroelectricity: electricity generated by waterpower.

impoverished: reduced to poverty; deprived of strength or vitality.

indigenous: originating in or characteristic of a particular region or country.

infrastructure: the system of public works, such as roads and sewers.

initiation: formal admission or acceptance into an organization or group.

kimberlite: a type of dark, coarse-grained rock that often contains diamonds.

militia: a body of citizen soldiers as distinguished from professional or career soldiers.

mutiny: rebellion against authority.

paramount: above others in rank; chief in importance; supreme and superior.

reconciliation: the act of bringing into agreement or harmony.

revenues: income collected from a given source.

sanctions: measures taken by a country to restrict trade and official contact with a nation that has broken international law.

savannas: plains characterized by coarse grasses and scattered tree growth.

sluggishly: slowly.

stifle: to suppress or end by force.

tributaries: streams that flow into a larger stream or other body of water.

turban: a headdress that involves winding a long cloth either directly around the head or over a cap.

More Books to Read

Beyond the Mango Tree. Amy Bronwen Zemser (HarperTrophy)

Folk Tales of Liberia. Steven H. Gale (Lerner)

Freedom Ships. Robert Caray, John F. Purbay (Af-Am Links Press)

The Land and People of Liberia. Mary Louise Clifford (Lippincott)

Liberia. Constance Morris Hope (Chelsea House)

Liberia. *Cultures of the World* series. Patricia Levy (Marshall Cavendish)

Liberia. *Enchantment of Africa* series. Allan Carpenter, Harrison Owen
    (Children's Press)

Libera in Pictures. *Visual Geography* series. Jo Mary Sullivan, Camille Mirepoix,
    Lerner Publicat Department of Geography (Lerner)

This Our Dark Country: The American Settlers of Liberia. Catherine Reef
    (Clarion Books)

Videos

Pavarotti and Friends for the Children of Liberia. (Uni/London Classics)

World History: Liberia: America's Stepchild. (PBS)

Web Sites

www.africanconservation.com/liberiaprofile.html

www.biodiversityscience.org/priority_outcomes/west_africa/upper.html

www.fol.org/

www.liberian-connection.com/tlc_animals.htm

www.liberianews.com/

www.pbs.org/wgbh/globalconnections/liberia/

Due to the dynamic nature of the Internet, some web sites stay current longer than
others. To find additional web sites, use a reliable search engine with one or more
of the following keywords to help you locate information about Liberia. Keywords:
Americo-Liberians, Joseph Jenkins Roberts, Liberia, Rubber, William Tubman, West Africa.

Index